Cognitive Behavioral Therapy

7 Steps to Get Free from Anxiety, Depression, Worry, Anger and Panic to find yourself again and Take Control of Your Life

By Practicing Mindfulness

By reading this document, the reader agrees that under no circumstances is the author responsible of any losses, direct or indirect, which are incurred as a result of the use of the information contained within this document, including, but not limited to, - errors, omissions, or inaccuracies.

Table Of Contents

Introduction

Cognitive Behavior Therapy is a form of therapy utilized for the mental treatment of regular mental and anxiety disorders. Since the 1980s, Cognitive Behavior Therapy or CBT, has been effectively used to treat individuals experiencing psychological issues, and is used to help them in living sound and completely working lives.

Cognitive Behavior Therapy is similarly as the name infers, a form of therapy utilized to treat cognitive zones of an individual's prosperity, and to change those cognitive regions such that it will at last change a person's conduct.

The good thing with CBT technique is that when you are in the middle of therapy, you have the opportunity to work hand in hand with your therapist so that you can identify the source of your negative thoughts. This is the best way in which you can transform these negative thoughts into positive ones, and hence, ultimately grow a positive mindset.

One thing that you have to understand with CBT is that the main goal is for you to replace those negative thoughts and behaviors with productive ones. Ask yourself 'Are these thoughts bringing out the best in me? Are my actions causing me more harm than good?' When you try to evaluate the impact that these feelings have on you and the people around you, you will be able to use CBT to equip yourself to overcome difficult moments.

In other words, you will use the technique to recognize how your thoughts influence your emotions. You will simply establish a rather personalized mechanism that will help you cope with the real-world-situation.

How does CBT work?

Well, so many people think that this technique is difficult, but trust me; it is one of the simplest ways in which you can overcome your problem. It works by helping you make sense of overwhelming issues by simply breaking them down into five major parts, namely:

- ➢ Situations
- ➢ Thoughts
- ➢ Emotions
- ➢ Feelings
- ➢ Actions

These five parts form the major concepts that underlie CBT. They are interconnected with each other and hence affect one another. For instance, when you face a particular situation, you begin to fuel thoughts about it, and this affects the way you feel; emotionally and physically. These feelings begin to take control of your physical body and hence influence how you act in response to the situation.

So many people wonder how this technique is different from other psychotherapies. Well, CBT is more pragmatic in the sense that it helps people identify the problems that they have and then helps them address them. It is also structured in that, instead of you talking about your life openly, you work with your therapist to discuss specific problems and then set goals for you to achieve while at it.

Additionally, CBT, unlike other psychotherapies, is focused mainly on the current problem. In other words, rather than trying to address issues that happened in the past, it aims at your thought process and your actions in response to them. In this case, the therapist will not tell you what to do, but they will work with you to identify solutions to your problems.

Using CBT to stop negative thought cycles

Did you know that there are helpful and unhelpful ways of reacting to a situation? Did you also know that your thoughts affect how you react to a situation?

Let us consider an example: if your marriage ends in divorce, the chances of you thinking you are the one to blame are high. You may even begin to think that you are not capable of a meaningful relationship. These thoughts might get the best of you and make you feel hopeless, depressed, lonely, and fed up. You then stop going out and hence, shutter your chances of meeting new people. You simply get trapped in a negative cycle where you feel bad for and about yourself.

Instead of accepting these thoughts, you should see your situation like any other marriage that has ended. Take that moment to reflect on what happened and learn from your mistakes and that of your partner. This way, you will not only come to terms with what has happened but also feel optimistic about the future. It is this kind of optimism that will fuel the social cues that will help you interact more with new people and better yourself.

Maybe your situation is not about divorce. It could be that you lost your job, closed your business or are facing some other problem. What you have to remember is that if you allow negative thoughts to cloud your mind, you will get trapped in negative feelings, sensations, and actions. This negative cycle will fuel new situations that will make you feel worse than you already do.

With CBT, you can stop these negative thoughts by simply breaking down that situation that is making you feel bad, scared or even anxious. In other words, it makes the whole situation manageable. It helps you transform each of these parts from negative patterns to positive ones, hence improve how you feel. It will help you transition from working with a therapist to working on your own in addressing problems you face every day with a high degree of success.

Exposure therapy

This is one form of CBT that is particularly aimed at helping people with the obsessive-compulsive disorder to deal with their issues. In this case, you have to bear in mind that talking about your problem is not very helpful. What is important is for you to learn to face your fears in a rather structured and methodical way through exposure.

You have to start with the things that bring you anxiety, but choose one that you can handle most easily. You then stay in this situation for an hour or two or until the time when you feel your fears and anxiety subsiding for a long while.

Most therapists insist on you repeating these exercises of exposure for at least three times each day. What is interesting is that, when you start facing your fears often, that anxiety begins to decline rather than increase, and will not last for very long.

You will then begin to gradually move to a more difficult situation. Then continue with the process until you have tackled all the things and situations that cause you panic and anxiety.

CBT Session

You can take part in a one-on-one session with your therapist or in a group of people dealing with the same issues as you are. If you choose to have a session with your therapist alone, you will have at least 5-20 sessions per week or fortnight. Every session will last from half-an-hour to one hour.

If you go through exposure therapy, one thing that you have to understand is that the sessions might be longer. The main aim of this is to ensure that you deal with anxiety hands-on so that it reduces by the end of every session. This may be in the clinic, outdoors, especially if you have specific fears, or in your home, especially if you have agoraphobia or OCD that involves certain items in your home.

What is important is for you to ensure that you are working with a professional who is trained in CBT. This can be a mental health nurse, psychiatrist or a psychologist.

Your first session

Before you can get all warmed up, the first thing is to determine whether CBT is the right mode of treatment for you. This upfront check ensures that you are comfortable during the process. In this case, your therapist will ask you a series of simple questions concerning your life and background.

In cases where you are struggling with anxiety or depression, it is important that you openly let your therapist know whether your issue interferes with your family, work and/or social life. You should also let them know about the events that you think are related to the problem, whether you have had treatment before and the objectives that you would like to achieve with the therapy.

If the CBT sessions are appropriate for you, it is important that you learn from your therapist what to expect during treatment. However, if CBT is evaluated to be inappropriate for your situation, or you do not feel comfortable with the process, you should work with your therapist to determine alternative treatments.

Further CBT sessions

Once you are through with the first session, start working with your therapist to break down your problem into various parts. To help you through this phase, your therapist will ask to keep a diary and notes on your behavioral patterns and thoughts, as well as their assessment of your progress.

During this time, you will both analyze what your thoughts, feelings and actions are like so that you can determine whether they are realistic and helpful when faced with a situation. The main aim of this analysis is to enable you to accurately determine what effects they have on you and each other. Then your therapist will help you work out ways in which you can change these thoughts and behaviors to improve your situation.

Once you know what you can change, you will have to practice the tips daily. Some of these include questioning thoughts that are upsetting and then replacing them with helpful ones; and recognizing when you are about to respond in a manner likely to make the situation worse rather than better.

To help with this exercise, it may be important to do homework sessions to help improve the process. Otherwise, during each session, it is important that you discuss with your therapist ways in which you have been able to practice these tips and come up with suggestions to help you further.

Remember that confronting your fears and anxieties can be tough, but your therapist will not ask you to do anything that you do not want to do. In other words, they will work at your pace so that you are comfortable with and during the sessions and the progress you are making. Once you are through with your sessions, the good thing is that you can keep applying principles that you learned to your daily life, hence lowering the chances of your symptoms recurring.

Types of Cognitive Behavior Therapy

It is evident that CBT utilizes some different approaches in addressing specific problems affecting people. Some of the types of CBT include:

Rational emotive behavior therapy (REBT)

This type of CBT is mainly focused on identifying any irrational beliefs that the patient might have and then trying to alter them. The process is characterized by first identifying the underlying source of the irrational beliefs, then actively challenging them and eventually learning ways to recognize and change these thoughts.

Cognitive therapy

This is a form of CBT that is mainly concerned with the identification of any distorted thought patterns, behaviors, and emotional responses; and then changing them.

Multimodal therapy

This is also a form of CBT that emphasizes that treatment of any psychological issue involves addressing seven distinct modalities that are interconnected with each other. These modalities include: affect, behavior, imagery, sensation, interpersonal factors, cognition, and biological aspects.

Dialectical Behavior Therapy (DBT)

This is also a variant of CBT that mainly pays attention to thought processes and behaviors of an individual by integrating such strategies as emotional intelligence and mindfulness in addressing them.

Step 1: Identify the problem

What Are Automatic Thoughts?

Automatic thoughts are a central aspect of the CBT theory. Automatic thoughts are those that come into our minds quickly, without effort. They are short and related to the specific situation at hand. They occur during or right after the situation, as an "instinctive" response. They don't include reflection or careful logic but usually seem quite reasonable. Some are perfectly logical; others are known as "dysfunctional automatic thoughts."

If you feel that another thought better connects to the problem, you can focus on that instead. Or if you feel that the issue underlying that particular automatic thought is not as important as other issues, you can set it aside and focus on other thoughts that had a stronger impact on your mood. When evaluating a series of automatic thoughts, assess how intense the feelings they stimulated were, and choose the thoughts that had the biggest impact.

Often, these types of dysfunctional thoughts result from cognitive distortions, or "thought traps," which are essentially mistakes we make in the thinking process. Automatic thoughts tend to fall into a few categories of cognitive distortions. Identifying the general patterns can be helpful in changing the thoughts that are a part of that pattern. It may be helpful to write down some of your automatic thoughts and then look for patterns. Below, we list some common types of cognitive distortions.

What Are Intrusive Thoughts?

Intrusive thoughts are another type of common but upsetting thought. Our brains generate many thoughts and ideas over the course of a day. Some feel completely normal, productive, and helpful, and we view them as reflective of who we are. Some thoughts may strike us as odd or confusing but are easily dismissed and don't cause much distress. We can also experience thoughts that seem bad, scary, or sickening—things that don't fit with who we are or that make us feel terrible, yet are hard to get rid of. These are known as intrusive thoughts.

Intrusive thoughts are thoughts, ideas, or impulses that are unwanted and upsetting but continue to occur. They are difficult to stop or control, which often makes them more distressing. They may interrupt activities and thought processes and cause feelings of doubt, shame, guilt, confusion, fear, and anxiety. Intrusive thoughts are common symptoms of anxiety disorders, obsessive-compulsive disorder (OCD), and post-traumatic stress disorder, but they can occur independently as well.

There are several types of intrusive thoughts, which may be treated in different ways. Obsessional intrusions usually relate to something that a person finds upsetting, disgusting, or repugnant, such as violence, taboo sexual acts, or his or her religious beliefs. These are often addressed within an OCD framework. Worry intrusions are anxious thoughts about future events or threats. Usually, dealing with anxiety through a range of CBT techniques will help reduce the frequency and severity of worry intrusions. Trauma-related intrusions are sudden recollections of past traumatic events. Addressing the feelings around these events with a therapist may help.

Trauma-related intrusions are sudden recollections of past traumatic events. Addressing the feelings around this event with a therapist may help.

Examples of Intrusive Thoughts:

Unwanted sexual thoughts involving a family member, child, or animal (obsessional intrusion)

Unwanted sexual thoughts involving a coworker whom you are not attracted to (obsessional intrusion)

Thoughts of committing a crime or violent act that you know you would never do, such as killing your spouse or harming your baby (obsessional intrusion)

Fear that you won't be able to stop yourself from saying something inappropriate in public (obsessional intrusion)

Worries that you no longer believe in your religion, briefly thought something forbidden, or performed a ritual incorrectly (obsessional intrusion)

Repeated, intensely felt doubts about your ability to perform on an upcoming exam you have studied for (worry intrusion)

Recurrent, distressing thoughts about contracting a rare disease and dying (worry intrusion)

Repeated thoughts about a humiliating event that happened in childhood (trauma-related intrusion)

Unwanted, upsetting recollections of a violent event you experienced as an adult (trauma-related)

These are just some of the many forms that intrusive thoughts can take. Many people are surprised to realize that others have experienced similar types of intrusive thoughts. Knowing this can be reassuring and help you reach a better understanding of intrusive thoughts as a common phenomenon, not a uniquely personal illness or failing.

Almost everyone has intrusive thoughts, but people respond to them in different ways. The key difference between people who do not struggle with their intrusive thoughts and those who do is not that the former do not have them, though they may experience them less frequently or intensely, but that they are able to dismiss upsetting, unwanted thoughts as meaningless. Those who struggle with obsessive thoughts tend to attach great significance to the thoughts and conclude that they really do believe or feel those things or really will commit those acts. They begin to build a narrative around the thoughts, with implications about their own character, behavior, and future actions.

The most important thing to understand about intrusive thoughts is that just having a certain thought or image *does not mean it is true.* Having an intrusive thought about an unacceptable violent or sexual action doesn't mean you actually want to or will commit the act. If you are religious, having a distressing blasphemous thought doesn't mean you truly believe it. Experiencing recurrent anxious thoughts about a future event does not mean that those fears are well founded or that the bad outcome is likely to occur.

Steven Phillipson, PHD, is a true expert in the field. He reminds his patients that they are not "mentally ill". Instead, they simply have an anxiety disorder. He also prefers to call intrusive thoughts "creative associations." This attitude encourages patients to embrace their experience of these common, if sometimes disturbing, thoughts. Find out more by searching "Dr. Phillipson OCD" in YouTube.

If intrusive thoughts are causing you distress, include them in the description of your problem.

Step 2: Getting familiar with anxiety and depression

To get a better understanding of how CBT works, we must get a clearer understanding of how our mind works in general. When we have thoughts, they usually fly through our minds in a tiny fraction of a second; quite often we don't even realize that we've had a thought, let alone the effects it has on our behavior.

So, when you lose a loved one in death, lose your job, deal with a family break-up, or have some other traumatic situation, you are quite likely to feel some level of sadness or even fear about what's in store for your future. These are pretty normal reactions to devastating events in our lives. We don't realize that these feelings and the behaviors that follow are a direct result of our thoughts. Most people will bounce back in time and get back to living life. However, for some, these low emotional states tend to be more intense and can linger for extended periods of time.

What is depression?

Depression, which tends to occur more in women than in men, is the direct result of these lingering thoughts. The way it manifests itself can vary depending on a person's age and gender. In men, it may be seen in symptoms such as tiredness, irritability, and sometimes anger. Men tend to behave more recklessly when they are depressed, which can be seen by their abuse of drugs or alcohol. These behaviors may often be passed off as masculine, so they are less likely to recognize it as depression and are not inclined to seek help or treatment.

Women in a depressed state are more likely to appear sad and have deep feelings of worthlessness and guilt. They may be reluctant to take part in social activities or engage with others, even those who are close to them. Depression in children will also be different. Young children may refuse to go to school or show signs of separation anxiety when parents leave. Teenagers are more likely to be irritable, sulky, and often get into trouble in school. In more extreme cases, you might see signs of an eating disorder or substance abuse.

There are various kinds of depressive disorders that could be remedied by CBT. The symptoms are often very similar in their degrees of intensity. If you recognize some of these symptoms in yourself or in someone you know, it is strongly recommended that you seek a professional diagnosis and start treatment as soon as possible, so you can get back to living a normal and productive life.

What is anxiety?

Closely associated with depression is anxiety, which can manifest itself in a variety of ways. A mild case of anxiety might be evidenced by the sensation of butterflies in the stomach in anticipation of an important event, concern about meeting deadlines, or nervousness about an anticipated treatment or procedure.

For most people, when anxiety is present, they can just ride it out. It is a normal part of life. However, there are some types of anxiety that are far from the norm. Some anxieties can trigger fears (spiders, snakes, planes, etc.) or phobias that are excessive and irrational fears.

To help in differentiating between normal anxiety and an anxiety disorder, first take a close look at the cause of the anxiety. Then look at the instinctive response to that fear. If the behavior is considered realistic, then it is probably 'normal' anxiety. However, if the response is viewed as extreme enough to disrupt normal life, it could be classified as an anxiety disorder.

For example, you may be anxious about getting sick, so you take steps to prevent illness. You may use hand sanitizer, regularly wash your hands, or even avoid shaking hands with people in public places. This is a normal form of anxiety. On the other hand, if your fear of getting sick is so strong that you don't want to leave your home or you are constantly washing and cleaning, you may have an anxiety disorder.

There are many different types of anxiety-related disorders out there, and for your convenience, these disorders have been grouped into three different categories:

- Anxiety disorders
- An excessive fear of a real or perceived threat
- Obsessive-compulsive disorders

- Intrusive fearful thoughts that trigger compulsive behaviors
- Trauma/stressor-related disorders
- The extreme reaction to a past traumatic or stress-related event

If you suspect you or someone you know has an anxiety disorder and is struggling to overcome the symptoms, CBT is one way to help. This method of helping patients identify the thought process that triggers the fear may be the best solution to the problem.

How CBT can help

By mastering the techniques in CBT, those with anxiety or depressive disorders can learn how to control those fears and the behaviors they trigger. The program will help to establish clear-cut goals to work on, teach them how to identify the thoughts that start the process, and arm them with defense mechanisms to fight these behaviors.

CBT helps by providing completely new ways to process those thoughts, feelings, and behaviors, so the patients can better cope with these normal events that happen in life. Instead of reacting negatively to traumatic events, it gives them the ability to reframe the triggering event and experience it from an entirely new perspective.

Identifying the Underlying Problem

In CBT, one of the first things you must do is to identify the underlying problem which triggers the negative and unwanted behavior. This is a crucial part of the therapy as it gives you an area to focus all your effort on. It also gives you purpose while you learn how to manage your feelings of anxiety and depression.

It is important to understand that people are not exactly alike, even if they have been diagnosed with the same disorder. This makes it very important that every CBT session is tailored to meet the unique needs of the individual. There is no blanket rule that will apply in every situation. For that reason, in order to identify the underlying cause for the negative behavior, you must first get a clear picture of how those negative thoughts fit into the entire picture of life.

In the initial visit with the therapist, you will probably be asked a series of questions. One of the first things you and the therapist will work on together is establishing goals. The therapist may not come right out and ask, "What are your goals?" or, "What do you want?" but instead may ask something less obvious, a question that will compel you to think deeply about your answer. For example, they may ask you what your reason is for seeking therapy, or why you feel you need help.

The reason for this is that we are rarely honest with ourselves. The first answer that comes to mind doesn't even address or identify the true nature of our problems. The real answers are often buried deep inside of us, and without some serious inward analysis of ourselves, the true answers may never actually come to the fore.

You could answer this question with the obvious. Many might respond with, "My wife told me to come," or, "I need help," but those answers don't really explain the real reason why you came. Chances are, if your wife told you to come, it is most likely because you are demonstrating certain behaviors she finds disturbing. This is a good reason for you to sit down and seriously consider why you're seeking out a therapist as that could be the first step in helping you get down to the root of your problem.

How to identify negative thought patterns when they present themselves

Chances are, even after the initial session, you may not have gotten to the core of your problem, but you will begin to think a little differently about identifying it. Whatever your problem is, you've gotten pretty good at covering it up, or you overcame it at some point. You also need to identify those tactics you used to handle your behavior, and the odds are high that if you look underneath these strong points you put forward every day, you'll find the root of your problem.

In this period of retrospection, it's important to take an honest view of your life and where you're heading. Look closely at how your anxiety and depression are affecting your behavior. Again, you have to start looking below the surface to reveal these behaviors, which may be obvious to other people, but it may not be so apparent to you. Your negative behavior may appear in different areas of your life.

Relationships

Some may be struggling with a difficult marriage. However, the underlying problem is not necessarily the marriage but in behaviors demonstrated in the marriage. If you're depressed, that may present itself as being very irritable, distant, or uninterested. Whether you're talking about a marriage, parent/child relationship, or a friendship, these kinds of behaviors over an extended period of time can really cause damage to a strong bond.

Anxiety also is not easily identified in your relationship. Without knowing how it is affecting you, it can be very difficult to see. Neither anxiety nor depression have clear signs that say, "I'm anxious or stressed," or, "This is me being depressed." They are hidden emotions that appear in a myriad of ways that affect your behavior.

You may have lost someone many years ago, friends moved away, lost some jobs, or trust was broken. These things do not have to be recent, as they can be experiences buried deep in your subconscious. However, since they were never addressed, these experiences are resurfacing to damage your present life.

Career

How you behave at work can reveal many things about yourself. Whether you're a work-at-home mom, or you're a corporate executive, if you have unidentified anxiety and depression, your relationships at work are going to suffer. Are you happy with your work? Do you wake up eager to get started, or do you feel like it is nothing but a tiresome chore, and you feel too unmotivated to perform your tasks?

Some people feel as if they are overworked, others may feel bored, and others may feel unfulfilled. Often, issues with money come up when thinking about work. You may thoroughly enjoy your work but are not satisfied because the money is not enough, or you may be working on a job that you hate because it pays the money you need. Understanding these things will help you identify the underlying problem hidden beneath the surface.

Spirituality

There is a big difference between having spirituality and having a religion. Many people feel this is the same and struggle with the inner self as a result. Religion is the belief of certain tenets, or teachings, whereas spirituality is what gives your life purpose.

How are you meeting that spiritual need? Most people find it by connecting to something more powerful than themselves, such as a 'supreme being of the universe.' Other people fulfill it through humanitarian efforts. If your spiritual self is not being fulfilled, it can leave you with a feeling of emptiness that no amount of money, relationship, or status in life can fill. Our personal sense of identity is closely connected to this, so it is well worth contemplating where we are in respect to our spirituality.

Physical well-being

Our physical health can also have an impact on our behavior. When we are not strong and healthy, it can have a deep impact on our emotions and mental state of mind. Even if we are relatively strong but are not physically active, it can have a strong negative impact on us. If you are dealing with chronic health problems, or you're just too busy to maintain your physical health, it could be the trigger to many of your negative behaviors.

Drugs and alcohol

Any kind of mood-altering substances can greatly affect your thought processes. If you find that you need to infuse yourself regularly with drugs, alcohol, or any other substance to get through the day, it could be a sign of depression or anxiety. Try to think if any of your family or friends pointed out that you might have a problem. Do you come home every day needing a drink? While you may not be an 'alcoholic,' as some may think, your depression or anxiety may have led you to develop a dependence on these substances in order to cope with the daily stress of life.

Food

Many people are stress eaters. They eat because they are stressed, unhappy, or bored. How does eating make you feel? Other people may have other fears that may be evident in their relationship with food. A poor self-image could cause you to not eat for fear of gaining too much weight. A poor self-image could also cause you to overeat, as you see it as comfort food, the only thing you have that makes you feel good.

Rest

The body is a highly efficient machine, but it can't run indefinitely. Like all machines, it needs to be refueled, and it needs to rest. If you're not getting enough rest every day or sleeping too much, this can cause problems. Some people naturally wake up the moment the sun rises, while others have to put up a struggle just to wake up. Others may fall asleep quickly but wake up in the middle of the night and cannot fall back to sleep again.

What keeps you from getting your rest? Is it the noisy dogs in the neighborhood, loud music, traffic, children, snoring, health problems, or worry? Many of these things could be perfectly normal, while others could be a sign of anxiety or depression.

Recreation

Everyone needs downtime from the rigors of daily life. If we have become so busy that we have no time to unwind or enjoy life, our mental state can suffer. Our brains and our bodies need to recharge to stay balanced. Many people who work second jobs to take care of their financial responsibilities or are constantly moving from sunrise to sunset so they can manage the necessary things in life, will eventually suffer from anxiety or depression.

If you have no free time or can't find time to slow down and relax, eventually, it will take its toll on you. Even if you have free time, but you can't let your mind relax, you are always thinking of the next task you've got to do, and you can't enjoy your break, this could be a trigger that is causing your negative behavior.

Hopefully, these points have made you look deeper into yourself and your behavior to help you identify the underlying triggers behind your negative behavior. After this type of contemplation, your mind is probably spinning in different directions. Now is the time to set some goals that will help you get your life back on track.

Step 3: Analyze the way you think and look the world

According to many psychologists, your past has a direct on your life today. We will explain how to know yourself and the various ways that your past influences your present behavior and how to handle your past presently.

How Your Past Affects Your Present

When you embark on a journey to know yourself in order to live a fulfilling life, you need to investigate the clutter in your past. Clutter in your past can act as the obstacles in today's life, hindering you from moving forward. Your experiences today are likely to have been influenced by your past experiences, as well. The way you act or interact with people today may be as a result of events in your childhood or young adulthood life.

It is important to understand the connection between your present and your past and how your past influences your future or present. All events, regardless of how big or small they were, are likely to influence your current life and your future.

Your personality and behavior today may be as a result of past experiences. When a child is born, they start collecting information from their environment and end up forming beliefs based on the information they gather. Psychologists say that children are able to absorb information so fast that by the age of 6 years they have formed some belies.

During your childhood and your teenage life, you are likely to have formed many beliefs, and these have influenced your personality and behavior today. The beliefs that you formed in your earlier life, they are likely to influence you negatively or positively. It is possible to change your negative beliefs and transform your life, although it is not easy and requires a lot of patience and discipline.

Change your beliefs to change your personality

You may ask yourself how it is possible to change your beliefs. First, begin by acknowledging the beliefs that have molded your personality over the years. After establishing them, it is time to dig into your past and identify what leads you to form those beliefs.

This is not easy to do because as the beliefs were getting formed you may not have been aware, hence you feel powerless over them. However, once you are able to get to the root of why you formed certain beliefs, it gets easier to deal with them. Identifying and understanding how they were formed is what gives you the power to break free from their hold. To understand it better, consider the following scene:

Suppose your boss complains that your performance was below average, and you did not deliver as expected. He says he expects better performance in the new month; will you want to know what went wrong and how it happened so as to fix it? The same way in your behavior, if you don't understand what caused you to behave in a certain way, then it will be impossible to change it. This is the main reason why in order to change and start living a better life free of negativity, identify your past influence of the mind. Know how it was formed and where it came from, then you can deal with the clutter conclusively by transforming yourself.

Examples

These few illustrations serve to show you how your past can shape your present.

If a boy grew up in a household that was violent, where he saw his father abuse the mother physically, and the mother accepted it, the boy may grow to believe this to be normal behavior. When he gets married, he is likely to be abusive to his partner because it is a norm for him and does not understand why his partner does not accept it.

A child that was abused will believe that he is worthless as compared to others because of how he was treated. This child grows up with low self-esteem and is likely to become very withdrawn and live with shame all his life. In his later life, he may become shy and scared that he may be abused again.

A last-born child is likely to receive a lot of attention all around him, and as a result, he develops a need to be recognized always. This need for attention will be with him, and when he becomes an adult, he may be very selfish and self-centered. The child may choose a career that puts him in the spotlight so that he remains the center of attention.

The above examples are just to explain how experiences in the past can cause a person to develop certain beliefs hence explaining their behavior and character in the present life. It is possible that you will not be aware of why you have a certain personality or behave in a certain way. If you truly desire to change your life for better, you need to purpose to change your mind from the negative beliefs.

Psychology- Understand, Accept, Heal the Past, Understand the Present

Every person has had a past with some people having more painful pasts than others or more pleasant memories of the past. Past experiences are known to influence your present life or behavior. Most painful pasts leave people with pain because of some traumatic experience they had. Some people even to deal with their painful memories opt to suppress them with the hope of forgetting the traumatic experience. They find themselves in destructive behaviors like overeating, anger issues, drinking, isolation, and many more. Healing from this is not easy; however, it is possible and doable. There are a few steps or strategies that will help you in your path, these are;

Evaluate your experiences – You must face it because you cannot deny it. Allow yourself to be open to thoughts, inner experiences, and feelings. Pick an aspect of your experience and meditate on it and notice what it makes you feel. You may notice you experience varied feelings or emotions towards it. This helps you increase your awareness of the incidence.

Be accepting and compassionate – as you meditate through your experience, try to understand it and empathize with it. This allows you to be compassionate towards yourself, and ease of your emotional challenges comes. This helps you understand the experience, accept it happened, and forgive yourself for it.

Take a break, it is important – It is not easy to face your pains and fears; in fact, it takes great courage but moves cautiously. Pay attention to the experiences do not rush through. When you feel overwhelmed by emotions, it is advisable to take a break; when you feel better, resume. The key thing is purposing to increase your self-awareness to a tolerable pace.

Calm yourself – To soothe yourself, learn how to mindfully breathe, focus on your breathing while blocking everything else out. You can also decide to engage in a positive activity like exercise that greatly relieves stress.

Bring it all together – this is the point where to heal past pain you must acknowledge its existence. Recognize the pain, accept it, and be compassionate towards it. You notice you start developing a deeper self-awareness over the experience while increasing your tolerance over it. As you progress, learn to recognize when you are approaching your limit of what you can handle and calm yourself down at that point. When you keep doing this, you realize you may not change how you relate to yourself, and your pain in the past may not change, but it will change your experience allowing you to forge forward with a more positive attitude in your life.

Recognize and Break Negative Thought Patterns

When a person forms a certain habit out of routine things they do, it can become a very powerful mental tool. Recognizing and treating an individual's thought process is not easy. When you cut yourself, you can easily use an anti-bacterial cream and bandage the wound, and in no time, you are good to go.

On the contrary, with negative thoughts, it is not as easy. If the negative thoughts stem from depression, anxiety, phobias, or other mental conditions, it becomes harder to change them.

Negative thoughts are compared to paper cuts that a person keeps forming when they have no idea of what is the cause for it. Sometimes a person will not realize they have negative thoughts until they begin to affect their lives.

Depending on an individual's triggers and condition, they will need various approaches to psychotherapy, medication, and lifestyle changes. If therapy is not included as part of the treatment, it may be difficult for a person to get quick treatment.

One way a person can break from their negative thought pattern is by gradually making a mental shift. In order to shift how you think, it will mean you are aware of the negative thoughts, and you make a conscious decision to change them.

Examine how you reflect on different situations or what you are thinking about the particular situation and switch your focus to something else. This calls for undoing negative behaviors and how one has programmed their mind through learned things. For instance, if as you were growing up, you were told that you must be the best in life and school, it is possible that you have programmed your mind for perfectionism. This can be very stressful, and making a shift mentally is a great way to fight against stress and anxiety. You must learn your most prevalent thought patterns, recognize negative thinking, and how you can redirect yourself and have constructive thoughts.

How do you Recognize Your Negative Thoughts

The "should" Thoughts

When you realize your thoughts are surrounded by the word "should," you need to stop and think. For instance, thoughts like:

I should feel better, or do or act,

I should exercise daily

I should change the way am eating

I should change the way I think

The intentions behind these thoughts are noble. Based on your situation, it would be healthier to exercise and eat whole foods. The word "should," however, can cause guilty thoughts and cause you to have more thoughts that are negative.

The ANTs

Apart from "should" thoughts, recognize other patterns that lead to automatic negative thinking. Behind the "should" statements, it is possible to have other cognitive distortions in negative thinking. These are called Automatic Negative Thoughts (ANTs).

When you have a strong reaction or feelings towards something, ANTs are your initial thoughts. They are more like reflexes rather than having freethinking. ANTs are learned and very persistent, mostly repeating themes like phobias or danger. ANTs are very common in persons with depressive or anxious thinking.

ANTs in individuals suffering from anxiety cause them to go on overdrive, turning their thoughts into serious panic attacks. Unfortunately, recognizing ANTs is not easy. Many people have had them all their lives and do not know it.

To recognize ANTs, however, you need to keep a thought record. Through Cognitive Behavioral Therapy, a person is encouraged to have a workbook to record these. The workbook is divided into three sections:

The current situation

Your attitude or moods towards the situation

What thoughts or image comes to mind at that moment?

Once you establish these, you must activate your thoughts into more productive ones that are wiser and helpful.

What is causing you to be anxious?

When you start recording your thoughts, you are actually putting your thoughts through a test. Begin by questioning yourself on what, who, where, or when. By doing this, it helps you describe what went on while ensuring you do not deviate from the facts to feelings. Some of the questions you can ask are:

- Who was with you?
- Which place where you at?
- What time was it?
- What activity were you engaged in?
- What is your attitude or mood in the situation?

Try and describe using one word what your mood or attitude was. Can you be able to rate your mood in a percentage? For instance, if you are at work and you needed to hand in a project, you may be feeling nervous, irritated, frustrated, or even guilty if you are not sure it is done very well. If you are nervous, this is what will determine your mood, and maybe you would rate it at 70%, and other feelings fill the remaining 30%.

Rating them is to help a person know how much the feelings affected their thoughts.

What traumatic thoughts run through your mind?

This is one of the most important things in recording your thoughts. You must record down the images and thoughts that immediately come to your mind concerning the situation. Remember your thoughts during the time. Some automatic thoughts that can pop up in your mind include:

- I am so stupid
- I Know I will just mess this up
- Everybody hates me
- This world is not a pleasant place
- I am unable to handle this
- I will always be lonely

If such ANTs are part of your thoughts, it may help to break down the situation into tasks and help you transform your mindset. For instance, check the reason why you believe that you are going to mess a situation before you start it. If it concerns work, try evaluating if the feelings you have are because of past projects that may have gone wrong. Imagine the worst-case scenario and establish your feelings about it. Analyze your moods and emotions and determine if the automatic thoughts or anxiety you are feeling are valid.

When you analyze keenly, it is possible to discover that the current situation has nothing to do with neither your experiences nor what you may face in the future. To gain control over your emotions, knowing what your automatic negative thoughts are is the best place to begin. Once you do this, it becomes easier to change them.

Changing Your Negative Thoughts

After identifying your automatic thoughts, you can put them to trial next. Think through and see if there is evidence supporting your thoughts. Establish if the evidence is from your past and how it applies to your current experience. Focus on credibility or facts but not on your emotions or thoughts or feelings. After this, turn your focus on evidence that does not offer your thoughts and support. For instance:

If your thought is: I will surely mess this up

Factual evidence for your thoughts:

My skills as a presenter are not the strongest

This is the first time am handling this size of a project along

Factual evidence against your thoughts:

For the past few weeks, I have practiced my presentation even in the presence of a colleague who gave me helpful tips

I understand the subject, and as such, I am able to handle any questions that may come up.

After establishing the factual evidence for and against your thoughts, it is now time to identify an alternative to the thoughts you first had. To do this successfully, try to remove yourself from the situation and assume you are passing judgment on behalf of your friend. Find a more balanced alternative thought that considers all the evidence and allow your mind to make a wise decision.

You can change your thoughts to think:

Yes mistakes have been made, but you are also a hard worker

In everything you do, you know you give your very best

Up to this point, I have always got positive feedback, and my supervisor trusts me.

As you do this, always remember to breakdown every situation into smaller, manageable tasks. Pause during the process and evaluate your thoughts and where you need to give yourself a break.

When you feel overwhelmed, acknowledging that fact is powerful and gives you the impetus to correct any negativity you may be feeling. Avoid putting yourself into a defensive mode that turns into an anxiety tailspin. Even when you feel anxious or stressed, welcome the mental strain positively in order to handle it effectively. Dreading the stress or anxiety may be more draining than accepting it. When you understand your anxiety and its cause, it is the first step into dealing with it effectively.

Establish if there is a trigger and try to avoid it as much as you can instead of dreading it. Instead of forcing positive thoughts in your mind, you can make small steps each moment you face some situations. Having a mental shift is not always about saying you feel sad, and immediately you feel happy.

As you go through the process, sometimes you will find it difficult to transform your thought pattern. However, being able to recognize and mention the thought, it can greatly help you towards having a shift to positivity. When you keep reminding yourself how to go about it, the easier it will get, and with time, you will realize you have no more negative thoughts.

Step 4 Set your goals and change your mindset

CBT teaches the importance of paying attention to behaviors and increasing the frequency of positive activities through Behavioral Activation. You have learned about the key elements of experience: thoughts, emotions, behaviors, and bodily sensations. You have learned the common Thinking Traps. You have started to learn how the Thought Record is used in CBT to connect automatic thoughts and feelings to particular situations that are arising in day-to-day life and how CBT defines a number of Thinking Traps that people commonly fall into. The fact that you have learned all this is already an accomplishment.

It is possible, however, to go a step further in your understanding of CBT. What you will now learn is how CBT teaches people actively to dispute automatic thoughts that involve Thinking Traps. But before we get into the details, it will help if you have some background on the cognitive model on which CBT is based. That way, you'll be in a better position to understand what it is a CBT client is trying to do when they are disputing their thoughts. Let's take a quick tour of the cognitive model.

The Cognitive Revolution

It wasn't too long ago that the computer was first invented. It was even more recently that computers became part of our everyday lives. Many of us can remember when the first personal computers first came on the market in the 1980s and 1990s. Since their invention, computers have changed many aspects of life and they have affected the way we think about ourselves.

One very big area of change occurred in psychology. Psychologists began to replace previous ways of understanding the mind and brain with a computer-based understanding. They started to think of the mind as functioning as a computer.

Most importantly, just as computers function to process information, so can the human mind. And just as computers can malfunction in processing information, so can the human mind - to better understand this idea, imagine a user who is using a computer to perform a basic arithmetic operation, like adding 2 + 2.

The user inputs "2+2" into the computer and it processes the input to yield an answer: "4."

Now imagine this same user who is faced with a broken, malfunctioning computer. She inputs "2+2" into the computer, but when it processes the input it outputs something false: "5"

Just as a computer can fail to process information properly, the human mind can also fail properly to process the information it is presented with. The development in psychology of thinking of the mind as a computer is known as the "cognitive revolution." This psychological revolution has allowed for new approaches to treating mental distress like depression and anxiety. Cognitive-behavioral therapy emerged out of this revolutionary new approach. CBT starts from the idea that common mental health disorders can be understood as the mind failing properly to process the information it is taking in.

The Cognitive Model of Anxiety and Depression

According to the cognitive model, anxiety and mood disorders are caused when the mind makes errors in processing information in the environment, resulting in higher levels of distress than is appropriate. Anxious and depressive states are sometimes normal - they become problems when they are triggered because our automatic thoughts are falsely causing these states to arise.

But it is not useful to you to become anxious in situations in which there is no likely threat. It is the mind that, like a computer, processes information about which situations are threatening to you, and which are not. In anxiety disorders, this information-processing function of your mind malfunctions. It is exaggerating the threat level that you face. For example, if you see a leashed miniature poodle at the other end of the park, and you feel a lot of anxiety, then there is likely a problem with the way that your mind is processing information.

In cases of anxiety disorders, the mind is operating like a smoke detector that is giving "false alarms."

Although it can seem odd to think of it this way, the ability to depressive responses can also sometimes be useful to us. Evolutionary psychologists have suggested that certain depressive responses can be normal reactions if we have invested our energy in a person or project, and then face a loss.

A period of low mood and detachment may actually help us to help the person to withdraw our investment in what we have lost so that they may go on to re-invest in new things and move on with our lives. You may be familiar with this idea if you have ever been through the "grieving process" that often happens after a major transition or loss.

But experiencing a depressive state is only useful to you if it is happening as part of a constructive process such as working through a loss.

It is not useful to you if you are becoming very depressed and there is no such process unfolding. According to the cognitive model, in depressive disorders, the mind is malfunctioning in the way it is processing information, making situations seem far more negative than they actually are. The minds of people who are depressed are known to produce a stream of negative thoughts that do not provide a full and balanced picture of the situations they are in. These include negative thoughts about themselves, others, the world, and the future.

For example, if someone who is depressed fails an exam; their thoughts may interpret the situation through an extremely negative lens as being one of hopelessness. By contrast, the thoughts of someone who is not depressed would provide a more balanced view of the situation.

Questioning Automatic Thoughts

Just as a malfunctioning computer can be reprogrammed, so can a human mind that is malfunctioning to create excessive anxiety or depression. To reprogram the mind, a person will need to deliberately attend to the way it is automatically interpreting situations in his or her life. That way, they can start a process of learning that results in forming new habits of thought - habits that are not as biased towards negative or catastrophic interpretations. There are two key ways to start to correct the automatic thoughts that distort the situation:

• By asking questions that dispute or challenge distorted automatic thoughts

• By carrying out "behavioral experiments" in which the person deliberately enters situations that will provide direct evidence against distorted automatic thoughts

According to CBT, there are some key questions that people can ask about their automatic thoughts in order to reprogram negative or catastrophic biases in their thinking.

•   What is the evidence in favor of, and against, my interpretation of the situation?

•   What is another way to view the situation?

•   Have I overlooked any important information about the situation?

•   Is the way I'm thinking helpful to me?

•   How might someone else (who is not already depressed or anxious) view the situation?

In a CBT program, the therapist asks the client questions like these to help them to challenge their automatic thoughts. This type of questioning is known as "Socratic" questioning, after the Ancient Greek philosopher Socrates. Socrates would ask people challenging questions in the course of philosophical analysis that would lead them fundamentally to rethink some of their basic beliefs. When someone is continuing with CBT on their own after they have finished working with a therapist, they are encouraged to continue to ask themselves challenging questions such as these. In this way, one goal of a CBT program is to eventually help people to become their own therapists.

Let's illustrate this process by considering how Sam begins to ask herself questions that challenge some of the automatic thoughts connected with her anxiety and depression.

Recall that, last week, when Sam woke up one morning and checked her email, she discovered an email from her manager. Right away, she started to panic and feel bad. Her automatic thought was "I must be in trouble." When she later found the courage to read the email, it turned out that her manager was asking about her return-to-work plan. Sam identified her Thinking Trap as Fortune Telling since she was anticipating a bad event (getting in trouble) but did not have direct evidence that this was going to happen.

We have already seen how Sam completed the first four columns of her Thought Record. Now we can focus on the last two columns. In these columns, she will dispute the automatic thought, "I must be in trouble," in order to arrive at a more balanced thought.

Notice the question Sam asks herself in disputing her automatic thought about being in trouble. She asks the first question listed above: What is the evidence in favor of and against my interpretation of the situation? Many people find it helpful to start with this question.

But the choice of which question or questions to ask is a matter of preference. Sam might have chosen instead to focus on the question "How might someone else (who is not already depressed or anxious) view the situation?" In that case, she might have brought to mind a friend or family member who is doing well emotionally, and who would have brushed off the email from the manager without taking seriously the possibility that they were in trouble.

To further illustrate the disputation of thoughts, let's consider a second example.

In this Thought Record entry, Sam decided to focus on the Thinking Trap of All-or-Nothing thinking. There might be other Thinking Traps, too (such as Fortune Telling or Mental Filter). But it is often helpful to focus on the one that stands out most prominently in the situation. In this case, Sam was struck by the way her automatic thoughts had made it seem to her that she was either all-good or all-bad at her job. In fact, the reality lies somewhere in-between.

Step 5: Be patient and confident with yourself

When it comes to anxiety, CBT has become one of the most effective treatment methods in the past few years. According to the research results, it has been seen that the effect of CBT can be seen in anxiety patients quite early after attending a few sessions. You will get a basic understanding of how CBT can be utilized to manage anxiety and the entire content is broken down into 5 simple steps or strategies.

Psycho-education

When someone seeks treatment for anxiety, they don't usually know about the problem much. They have very limited knowledge and due to this, some patients may even end up making assumptions about anxiety which are partly or completely wrong. All that the patients are completely sure of is what makes them anxious. But if the problem is complex or the underlying cause of anxiety is something way deeper than what meets the eye, then pin-pointing the cause of anxiety can be a difficult task as well. On the other hand, there are others who might be facing anxiety their whole life without even being aware of its presence.

So, the first and foremost thing that you should do in order to manage anxiety is to learn about it. This process of learning about the problem, in general, is called psycho-education. When you learn more about your problem, you'll get a feeling of comfort that you are not alone in this fight and that what is happening to you is not something abnormal. Moreover, when you learn that there are helpful strategies that you can use to combat your problem, you will automatically feel more reassured.

If you are not sure where to start, then starting off with identifying the sources of your anxiety or the triggers would be a good idea. Which are the situations that push you to become anxious? What do you feel in such situations or how do you respond? You should also start educating yourself on how these situations are placing an impact on your life. So, once you have answered questions related to your own anxiety, start knowing a bit more about anxiety in general. According to the definition in books, it is a feeling of general discomfort which makes people avoids their triggers at all costs. Avoidance lies at the base of anxiety.

The most basic concept that you need to understand with respect to anxiety is that the more you avoid it, the further it will intensify. So, when you avoid your anxiety-producing situation the first time, you will definitely feel better (at least that's what it will seem like from outside) but the next time you face that same situation, every feeling is going to increase by ten folds. So, the graph keeps escalating in this manner until and unless you find a solution.

You should learn more about the *Yerkes-Dodson Law*. When you study this law, you will understand how anxiety is rooted in your thoughts and how it is causing all the problems in your life. The law also shows how and why anxiety can be helpful when present in certain amounts. According to the law, when the level of anxiety in a person is too high or too low, it can be dangerous but with the presence of a moderate level of anxiety, the person will be able to show optimal performance levels. The underlying concept of this law is that when a person does not have any anxiety at all, it usually correlates to not having an ounce of motivation in life. On the other hand, too much anxiety causes avoidance. But with a moderate level of anxiety, the person will be able to concentrate on their goals and take measures to achieve them without taking a step back or becoming intimidated.

Challenge Your Negative Thoughts

Understanding cognitive distortions is a major part of CBT. These are nothing but the thought patterns in a person that cause all the problems and lead them to be unhappy. Some of the most common patterns include black and white thinking, catastrophizing and overgeneralization. The list of such cognitive distortions can be exhaustive and you will often notice that the list can get overlapping too. The following example should make the concept clearer.

Suppose a teenager who is currently in high school rethinks whether she should attend the high-school dance or not. This doubt comes in her mind because she thinks that the moment she attends that dance, people will laugh at her and she will feel humiliated. She also is anxious about the fact that it will become difficult for her to show her face to someone else in her high school ever again. From this example, it is clear that she is suffering from anxiety about social interaction. And due to this feeling of anxiety, she feels that people will laugh at her and this feeling is known as emotional reasoning. Besides, she also concludes that she will be humiliated when she attends the party. This can be categorized as catastrophizing, magnification and jumping to conclusions.

If you examine the above example carefully then you will also see how black and white the girl's thoughts are. She has set all the positive outcomes on one side and she has never even considered them to be true. Instead, she anticipates that all her experiences will be negative or bad and that there is zero potential for anything good to be happening. All of these conclusions arise from the basic feeling of anxiety that she has but emotional reasoning is the dominant cognitive distortion present here. And in reality, this is also one of the most commonly noticed distortions in people as a tendency to derive false conclusions based only on feelings is quite common in people.

So, what can you do to ensure rationality when there is so much cognitive distortion based on your emotions? Of course, there is no easy way out of this as you continually keep trying to sabotage your own good feelings because that path is way easier. You might have had a long-held belief or approach that promotes negative thinking and questioning that belief will be difficult. But CBT is all about distancing yourself from your own thought processes so that you can see and judge it all from a third-person perspective. In this way, you will gradually learn how you can test the validity of your thoughts. You will also be able to challenge the significance of all those negative outcomes you fear the most. So, challenging your thoughts is a very important exercise in your fight against anxiety and doing it on a daily basis is crucial.

Implement Exposure Therapy

It is very common among anxiety patients to avoid certain situations mostly because it gives them short-term relief from the problem. But it is not a solution. As already mentioned before, avoidance will only make things worse. That is where exposure therapy comes into play. The idea of exposure therapy is based on the fact that anxiety patients should face their problems in order to combat their problems. When the person starts exposing themselves to the triggers or the situations that lead them to become anxious, they start noticing how everything is not as bad as they thought it to be. So, with time the anxiety lessens.

But this does not mean you overexpose someone. For example, if someone has a fear of spiders, you do not just lock them up in a room full of spiders. Then what should you do? You should proceed with systematic desensitization which means you will gradually expose them to their feared stimuli and not do anything all at once. You know that the first step of exposure therapy

is the creation of a fear hierarchy. For the above-
mentioned example, you can create the hierarchy in the
following manner:

Listen to a story that revolves around a spider or has
something to do with a spider

Hold a picture of a real-life spider or keep it on your
arm

Keep a spider in a cage and sit in a room with the cage
placed near you

Take out the spider from the cage but make sure it is at
a certain distance from you

Place a harmless spider on your hand and let it walk

If you want to learn how you can manage your anxiety
effectively, you need to learn how to expose yourself to
it. You have to practice getting exposed to these triggers
on a regular basis in small doses until and unless you
become comfortable with each step.

Acquire Relaxation Skills

Relaxation skills are something that you should learn if you plan to perform exposure therapy. You should not start the therapy until and unless you have mastered these skills. These skills will help in bringing a calming response in your body once you have been exposed to the stimuli. There are different types of relaxation skills that you can master and what works for some other person may not work for you. This is because every person is different and so you need to figure out which relaxation strategies work best for you. Some of the common ones are listed below.

Slow Diaphragmatic Breathing

This is one of the best skills that are used in the case of CBT. You must have been told at least once in your life to take a few deep breaths whenever you were tensed. The basic concept of this strategy is that whenever you slow down your breathing, the anxiety response of your body also changes accordingly. A slower pace of breath automatically signals your brain that situations are safe. The process requires you to take conscious control of how you are breathing. Here is how you can practice this strategy:

Keep your feet on the floor and sit on a chair in a comfortable position. If you feel more comfortable while lying down then you can do that as well.

Keep your hands folded on your abdomen.

Breathe calmly and slowly. Take a normal breath that will fill up your belly. Do not stress on breathing heavily. When you are breathing in, your belly should fill up like a balloon. But you must remember that the pace of your breath is more important than the depth. Breathe into your stomach and don't let your shoulders get lifted while you are breathing.

Count till 5 and breathe out at a slow pace. The exhaling rate should be slowed down as much as possible. Before you inhale again, take a break of 2-3 seconds.

Continue the process in the exact same manner for about 10 minutes.

If you want the best results, then you should practice the same at least twice a day on a regular basis.

Progressive muscle relaxation

Although this relaxation strategy requires a greater level of effort than that required in slow diaphragmatic breathing, it is, beyond doubt, quite helpful in reducing levels of anxiety. The main idea behind this strategy is to teach you how releasing tension from your muscles can be achieved with the help of exercise. In order to perform this exercise, you can first begin with flexing your biceps. Maintain this position of increased muscle tension for at least a period of 7 seconds. Now let go of the flexing and drop your arm to your sides. You will be able to notice the difference as the relaxed feeling in your arm starts kicking in. The blood will gradually flow into your arms giving you a feeling of warmth. You can perform the same exercise with each set of muscles that are present in your body but this has to be done on a daily basis as well.

Start Thinking Realistically

Do you pay attention to your own thinking process? Well, most people don't. But you should because your thoughts affect every action. If you want to effectively track the type of thoughts that you are having, you should pay more attention to your thinking process. This is often termed as self-talk.

Now that you are more aware of the impact of your thoughts, you should spend more time in order to identify the negative thoughts or the thoughts that are causing unhappiness. You need to start thinking realistically about your thoughts because not all negative thoughts are meant to be challenged and sometimes people face difficulty in identifying the thoughts that actually need challenging. For example, if your mother is suffering from some serious illness and you are sad because of it, then it is completely normal and this thought does not require to be challenged. On the other hand, if your friend didn't show up at a date and you end up thinking that there is something wrong with you and feel anxious about social interactions, then that thought definitely needs to be challenged. No matter how small the change in your emotion is, don't ignore it. Find the root cause of that change and examine it with realism.

So, once you have identified the negative thought that has been bothering you, your next step would be to come with positivity and realistic thoughts that will keep you going. You need to form your own positive self-statements and coping statements. If it helps then you can also try and write down your coping statements on a piece of paper. Keep this paper with you at all times so that even if you feel anxious, you can simply take it out and read the statements in order to feel positive.

The stage for anxiety is set up with isolation and loneliness. If you want to become less vulnerable to anxiety then you should start socializing and speaking with your near and dear ones. And if you are feeling anxious about social interaction, then you use the above 5 methods to gradually overcome your hesitation. Make positive choices whenever you can. There should be a positive mental outlook in everything you do and make it a point to eradicate negativity from all aspects of your life. Make a conscious decision on a daily basis to promote positivity and relaxation.

It is true that there is no quick fix to this. There is no shortcut. It takes both your commitment and time to finally be able to overcome your anxiety issues. But you should stick to your therapy along the entire journey. If the pace of our recovery is demotivating you, then you must remember that it is the result in the long run that will actually be huge and prominent not what you see in the short-run. Stress is also a factor that adds up to your anxiety problems so say no to stress. Don't overburden yourself with responsibilities that you cannot take. Look for ways that will help you lessen the stress. Make time for recreation, go watch movies, and simply read a book. Do whatever makes you feel happy and relaxed. In short, keep some 'me' time for yourself in your daily schedule.

So, if you are someone suffering from anxiety, follow thoroughly and you will see gradual improvement with every step that you take.

Step 6: Maintain Mindfulness in your life

We dive into mindfulness, the "third wave" in CBT alongside cognitive and behavioral practices. Mindfulness has emerged in the past few decades as a powerful way to maintain our equilibrium as we deal with difficult emotions.

Matt didn't know how much more of this he could take. For the past few nights he'd been working to transition his infant daughter to falling asleep in her crib rather than while being rocked, and it wasn't going as smoothly as he'd hoped.

"She should be asleep by now," he thought to himself as his daughter continued to babble away. He had gone into her room once already to resettle her and thought she was close to drifting off when he left. But a minute later he heard her very awake-sounding voice through the baby monitor. A few minutes later her babbles turned to crying. Matt knew he'd have to settle her again.

He shook his head as he entered her room, hoping she couldn't sense his irritation. He looked forward to finally getting to watch his TV show in peace as he patted her back, rolling his eyes and gritting his teeth in the darkness.

What Is Mindfulness?

If you pay attention to what your mind is doing, you'll notice two strong tendencies:

1 **The mind focuses on things other than what is happening right now** - Most of the time we're thinking about events that have already happened or that might happen in the future. Thus our well-being is often affected by things that have little to do with the moment in which we find ourselves.

2 **The mind continually evaluates our reality as good or bad** - It does so based on whether things are working out the way we want them to. We try to cling to circumstances we like and push away those we dislike.

These tendencies are part of what it means to be human. They can also cause us problems and needless suffering. Focusing on the future can lead to worry and anxiety, most often about things that will never happen. Ruminating on events from the past can lead to distress and regret about things that are no longer in our control.

In the process, we miss the once-in-a-lifetime experience that each moment offers. We don't really take in the people around us, the natural beauty of our surroundings, or the sights, sounds, and other sensations that are here right now.

Our constant and automatic effort to judge things as either for us or against us also creates unnecessary pain. We often end up resisting things we don't like, even when such resistance is futile. A perfect example is raging against the weather—no amount of cursing the rain will make it stop, and we'll only frustrate ourselves in the process.

The practice of mindfulness offers an antidote to both of these habits.

Presence

Mindfulness is as simple as bringing our awareness to the present. That's it - If you're walking the dog, pay attention to that experience - If you're having lunch, focus on having lunch. If you're arguing with your partner or embracing afterward, be fully in that experience.

Sometimes when we learn what mindfulness is we say, "I already **know** that I'm walking the dog. I know I'm having lunch. How is that supposed to be helpful?" But mindfulness is more than knowing **that** we're doing something. It's about going deeper, intentionally cultivating a connection with our experience. We don't **just** walk the dog—we notice the color of the sky, the feel of the ground under our feet, the sounds our dog makes, and the periodic pulls on the leash. It's opening our awareness to elements of our experience that we normally miss.

At the same time, a mindful approach doesn't require that we do anything in addition to what we're engaging in. If we're running, we're running. If we're driving, we're driving. People sometimes protest that being mindful in certain situations would be distracting, even dangerous. In fact, the opposite is true—we're safer and less distracted when our attention is fixed on what we're doing.

Simply being present in our lives accomplishes two things at once. First, it allows us to get more out of what's happening, so we don't sleepwalk through our lives. We can discover the richness in our reality, even in the most mundane activities. Second, when we're present, we're not ruminating about the past or fearing the future, which is a big part of why mindfulness practice reduces anxiety and depression.

So much of our unhappiness arises from things that have nothing to do with what's real in this moment. For example, I was walking home from the train one evening and started thinking about my children's health. Before I knew it, I was imagining a tragic scenario in which one of them was gravely sick, and I began to feel anxious and downcast as though it were already happening. When I caught myself and came back to the present, I noticed what was real: the lengthening light, the birds flying, the green grass, and blue sky. My kids were healthy as far as I knew. I didn't have to live in my tragic fantasy. It was hard not to smile with that realization as I headed home to see them.

Acceptance

The second core feature of mindful awareness is acceptance, which means opening to our experience as it unfolds.

After a couple miserable nights, Matt realized he needed a new perspective on his daughter's bedtime. The next night he decided to try a different approach—what if he let the night play out however it was going to? It's not like his resistance made things better: it was making him frustrated toward his baby every night. He resolved to do his best to help her fall asleep, and to release his fierce attachment to controlling exactly when that happened.

The first time his daughter began to cry, Matt took a calming breath before going into her room. Instead of telling himself, "I hate this," or, "This is ridiculous," he thought, "This is what's happening right now." Then he took stock of what that statement actually meant: He was standing by the crib of his baby girl, whom he loved more than words. He was patting her tiny back, which was the size of his hand. He could hear her breathing begin to slow. He realized how in that moment he had no real complaint about anything. He wasn't cold, hungry, thirsty, or in danger. His daughter was healthy. She just wasn't asleep yet. Maybe things were exactly as they ought to be.

Matt's example reveals important corollaries of mindful acceptance. First, it doesn't mean we stop having preferences for how things go. Of course, Matt still wanted his baby to fall asleep quickly and easily, and wanted to have more of the evening to himself to unwind. Accepting meant holding those preferences more lightly, and not assuming his daughter was doing something wrong by not being asleep when he wanted her to be.

Accordingly, Matt didn't throw in the towel and stop following the bedtime routine he and his wife had agreed on to transition their baby to falling asleep on her own in her crib. He stuck to his plan, offering predictability and consistency while recognizing that he couldn't control his daughter's sleep.

When we stop fighting against the way things are, we relieve an enormous portion of our stress. Earlier in my career I had a very difficult supervisor, and I often found myself tied up in my thoughts as I tried to make sense of how unreasonable she was. Finally, I reached a point of accepting that she could just be difficult, period. My acceptance didn't change her behavior, but it did free me from acting as if she were doing something surprising. She was simply being true to form.

A crucial part of acceptance is that it lets us respond appropriately to the facts in front of us. My acceptance of my boss's temperament made it clear to me that I needed to find work elsewhere, which underscores the distinction between acceptance and apathy.

Benefits of Mindfulness

Training in mindfulness helps with a wide range of conditions. A partial list includes anxiety, attention deficit/hyperactivity disorder (ADHD), chronic pain, depression, eating disorders, excessive anger, insomnia, obsessive-compulsive disorder (OCD), relationship difficulties, smoking cessation, and stress. Many treatment programs have been developed that integrate mindfulness practices into CBT. One of the first was mindfulness-based cognitive therapy (MBCT) for depression, developed by psychologists Zindel Segal, John Teasdale, and Mark Williams. These developers reasoned that the tools of mindfulness were well suited to remedy some of the factors that contribute to depression. For example, practicing paying attention to one's internal experience could strengthen one's ability to detect early warning signs of depression, like unrealistic negative automatic thoughts.

MBCT includes elements of traditional CBT for depression and integrates training in mindfulness to protect against relapse. Much of the training focuses on using mindful awareness to notice problematic thoughts. It also emphasizes learning a different relationship with our thoughts. We can learn to recognize them as simply thoughts rather than something we need to react to.

Multiple studies have shown that MBCT achieves this aim. For example, a study by Teasdale, Segal, Williams, and their colleagues found that among individuals with recurrent depression, MBCT reduced the risk for relapse by nearly half versus the comparison group that received treatments other than MBCT (e.g., antidepressant medication, other types of psychotherapy).

Acceptance and Commitment Therapy (ACT), developed by Steven Hayes, has also received strong research support for treating several conditions like depression, anxiety, and chronic pain. As the name suggests, it emphasizes acceptance of our experience in the service of committing to action that supports our values. Closely related to ACT is Acceptance-Based Behavioral Therapy, designed by Susan Orsillo and Lizabeth Roemer to treat generalized anxiety disorder. And the best-tested treatment for borderline personality disorder—a debilitating and difficult-to-treat condition—includes a strong mindfulness component to address the difficulty handling the strong emotion that is part of this diagnosis. Mindfulness clearly has beneficial effects on many psychological issues. How does this approach lead to improvements?

How Mindfulness Helps

There are several ways in which mindfulness practice produces its benefits:

Greater awareness of our thoughts and emotions - When we practice paying attention more and opening to our reality, we begin to know ourselves better. We give ourselves the space required to recognize how we're thinking and feeling and, because we accept reality as it is, we don't deny our own experience.

Better control of our emotions - Greater awareness of our internal experiences helps us interrupt unhelpful trains of thought like rumination and resentment. Adopting a present focus also tends to be calming, which can loosen the grip of runaway emotions.

A different relationship with our thoughts - Our minds are continuously generating thoughts. As we allow these thoughts to come and go during mindfulness practice, we start to give less weight to them. We learn that they are simply ideas created by our minds, and not necessarily a reflection of anything meaningful.

Decreased reactivity - As our relationship with our thoughts evolves, we become less prone to habitual reactions, which are often not in our best interest. Mindfulness can provide a pause before we act on our initial impulse, giving us enough time to choose a response that fits our goals and values.

How Can We Practice Mindfulness?

Like any habit, being more mindful takes practice. There are two major categories of mindfulness practice: activities designed specifically to engage mindful awareness and bringing mindfulness to our ordinary life activities.

Formal Mindfulness Practices

The most common formal mindfulness technique is sitting meditation. It involves choosing something to focus on for a set amount of time and opening to the experience as it unfolds moment by moment. The most common target of focus is our breath, which is always with us and always happening in the present. Inevitably our attention will drift to other times and places, or we'll start engaging in judgments of how we're doing or whether we like meditating. The practice is simply to return to our intended focus once we realize we've lost it. This focus on coming back to our present moment, without criticizing our minds for wandering, is the essence of meditation.

Other common types of meditation can entail a focus on bodily sensations (body scan meditation), ambient sounds, or wishes of health and contentment toward ourselves and others (loving-kindness meditation).

Formal practices also include more active exercises like yoga and tai chi. In yoga, for example, we can pay attention to the physical sensations of the poses, including the breath that's synchronized with our movement. We can also practice acceptance of the discomfort we sometimes feel in challenging postures, which can lead to either staying in the pose and breathing with the discomfort or changing our position if necessary. Awareness and acceptance promote choice.

Loving-Kindness

How to Start Meditating

The idea of meditation is simple, but the practice of it typically is not easy. When we sit down to meditate, the mind often decides it has other things to do. Common reactions when we start to meditate include:

• Feeling a bit bored

• Feeling frustrated

• Wanting to stop

• Suddenly remembering things you've been meaning to do

• Having countless thoughts clamoring for your attention

None of these experiences means you're doing something wrong or can't meditate, so stick with it. It can help to keep the following things in mind for your meditation practice:

You're not bad at meditating - We'll lose our focus again and again while we meditate. If you think you're bad at it, think again—meditation is simply re-finding our focus as many times as we lose it. We don't have to buy into the self-critical thoughts that intrude into our meditation sessions.

The goal is not to "become good at meditating" - It's easy to bring the habit of judging to our mindfulness practice, which can make meditation both punishing and disappointing. The point of meditation is simply to focus on the present and to let go of judgments.

Let go of attachment to a specific outcome - You probably have expectations of what meditation will be like—having a clear and settled mind, for example—and could strive to make the experience match what you expect. But in reality, we never know what we'll experience during meditation. We can practice opening to whatever happens in a particular session.

There are many ways to meditate. Here's a simple plan to get started:

1 Practice meditation when you're able to stay awake and alert.

2 Find a quiet place where you won't be disturbed, and remove possible distractions like your phone.

3 Choose a comfortable seat on the floor, in a chair, or anywhere else. If you sit on the floor, you can raise your hips with a blanket or a yoga block if that's more comfortable.

4 Close your eyes if you wish, or keep them open and fixed on the floor a few feet in front of you.

5 Practice with or without a recording; set a timer if you do it without. Five minutes is a good starting point. Keep the timer out of sight.

6 Begin to notice the sensations of breathing, paying attention to them for the full length of your inhalation and exhalation.

7 Bring your attention back to the breath each time you realize your mind has wandered.

8 There are many apps and free online meditations available if you prefer a guided meditation. Aura and

Insight Timer, for example, are free meditation apps available for iOS and Android systems.

Finally, as with anything else, maintain a light touch. Meditation practice is for you, so beware of making it yet another chore to cross off your list.

Step 7: Move forward without looking back

Many studies have found that your attitude makes the difference between achieving success and becoming a failure. You might be a very qualified individual, but if your attitude is nasty, you will end up achieving less than an under-qualified person with a great attitude. In many fields of work, success is down to the collaborative skills of individuals, and if you have a poor attitude, you will make a poor teammate.

A negative attitude is a psychological impediment to success, but even worse, it makes people shun you. If you have a terrible attitude, you are going to have a terrible time of it. Thankfully, your poor attitude is not set in stone. You can change it if you choose to.

The following are some of the secrets of developing a warm attitude that will draw people in and also open you up to opportunities:

Stop Acting Entitled

When you act entitled, you send the message that you have too high an opinion of yourself. This will antagonize other people, and you will have zero allies.

When you are on good terms with people, you have the best environment for cultivating a great attitude.

Be Grateful

If someone shows you kindness, the least you can do is appreciate their effort. People notice those who never appreciate their kind gestures. It reeks of entitlement. Be grateful in small and big things alike. It will help you establish connections and enter into mutually beneficial relationships.

Improve Your Lifestyle

Your lifestyle has a great influence on the person you end up becoming. If you're into binge drinking and spending your weekends laughing around with female or male hookers, it would be quite challenging to develop a great attitude. A great attitude goes together with a certain awareness of a moral compass. So, cut out the drunken weekends, and channel that time into spending time with your loved ones. Another important aspect of your lifestyle is your diet. Cut out the junk and start preparing healthy meals. Healthy meals are not only good for your emotional and mental health but also your wallet.

Reframe Your Challenges

Regardless of the challenges that you might be facing, never assume a rigid approach. Look at your challenges from various angles. The more flexible you are, the more creativity you stir in yourself, and ultimately, you will be in a far better position to solve your challenges.

Embrace Rejection

Harden your heart a little bit so that rejection won't cripple you. The fact of the matter is that on the path to reaching your goals, you are going to get rejected more times than you will care to remember. Read about movie stars and the rejection that they go through. When you learn to embrace rejection, you elevate yourself into the mindset of an unstoppable winner.

Use Positive Words

If you have a negative attitude, it follows that negative words will escape your mouth when describing your life. You will always come from a perspective of lack and misery. Change this pattern by starting to say positive things about yourself. Look at your glass as half full – not half empty.

Become a Doer

Instead of talking about the grand plans that you haven't acted upon yet, make a rule of talking about the things you have actually done. This will push you into becoming more of a doer than merely a talker. For instance, instead of saying, "I'll drop my CV to twenty offices this week," it should be, "This week; I dropped my CV to twenty offices."

Become Wary of Energy Vampires

Sadly, not everyone in your life is well-meaning. Various people act like a vampire – they drain your energy. When you discover an energy vampire, you want to pull away from them as quickly as you can, so that they don't deplete your positive energy.

Deep Breathing Exercise

There is a direct relationship between our breathing and our emotions. When we are constricted and have trouble breathing, we become susceptible to negativity. However, when we inhale oxygen-rich air on the regular, we tend to become grounded. Practice deep-breathing exercises and watch your negative thinking patterns fade away.

Choose to See the Positive Side

No matter how bleak the situation appears, always choose to see the brighter side of things. If your company posts losses, don't wallow in despair but choose to see it as an opportunity to prove your mettle. If your company posts massive profits next year, you will reclaim your top spot, and inspire others. Always choose to see the bright side of things.

Be More of a Problem-Solver

A negative person points out problems for the sake of tearing things down. They rejoice in bringing people down to their level. But you should place as much thought into the solution as you place into the problem. Instead of criticizing and leaving it at that, offer a solution, and the other party will appreciate your criticism.

Become the Agent of Joy

There is no shortage of sadists in the world. However, there aren't enough people to spread joy, which is what we need more of. Become the agent of spreading joy around the world. When you have a positive impact on the lives of people, it increases your self-esteem and challenges your natural selfish tendencies.

Cultivate Meaningful Relationships

When you're in a relationship, you learn to become a giver, not always a taker. Being selfless is a vital element of a positive attitude. As a giver, you operate from the mindset of abundance, and this leads you to become a resourceful person.

Develop Crisis Management Skills

Whatever happens is not the actual problem, but your reaction is where the problem is. You cannot escape crises for as long as you are alive. However, if you have crisis management skills, you are far more likely to emerge out of the situation unscathed, and yet preserve your good image.

How to Practice CBT in your Every Day Life

Low-level Physical Exercise

low-level physical activity can offer some great benefits, and I recommend that you use this type of exercise as much as you like, as long as your body is okay with it. These types of exercises are least likely to worsen stress. Instead, they should feel very relaxing.

Low-level physical exercise can be a walk, a yoga session, an easy bike ride, a hike, or anything else that isn't very physically challenging. Doing low-level physical exercise every day can be perfect for your stress levels and it doesn't have to be that difficult. All you have to do is walk around for a bit (preferably in nature).

Resistance Training

If you have the energy for it, doing some resistance training once in a while can be very good for your resilience to stress and your overall health.

Resistance training is when your body pushes against a force. The most common types of resistance training are weight lifting and other types of strength training. It sounds stressful for the body to do some heavy weight lifting, you might think. And you would be completely right. However, it is a bit more complicated than that.

Resistance training does put some stress on your body in the short term. This is not necessarily a bad thing if you have a proper routine, though. The key to appropriate training of resistance routine is enough recovery time. I recommend six to nine days. When you do resistance training this way, you will make your body momentarily stressed after the exercise. However, when you allow your body to recover for six to nine days, it will increase your resilience to stress in the long term. So, when you follow this routine, you exchange some short-term stress for long-term stress relief and resistance.

However, if you're already very stressed, you might not want the temporary stress increase from resistance training. That's why I recommend that you only do resistance training if you feel like you have enough energy to do it. If you do, it can be very beneficial for you and make you more resilient to stress over time.

Aerobic Exercise

Aerobic exercise is very popular, and it can be beneficial. However, it can also require a lot of effort and time, which can be quite stressful.

Aerobic exercise, also known as endurance training or cardio, can be something like running, swimming, or cycling. Or it can be almost any sports that require constant movement. If you have an existing practice of this type of exercise that you like, you can keep doing that. Especially if it also includes good social relationships - however, aerobic exercise is typically not the first type of exercise that I would recommend for people with chronic stress issues. That's because endurance training is frequently seen as something you must do every day, or at least three to four times a week, for 30-60 minutes to get good results. This can be a lot of time for you to invest, which you really don't have to. Plus, it can be very taxing for your body and just put more stress on it. Also, you don't have to do aerobic exercise for several hours every week to see excellent benefits from your exercise routine.

Like I said, if you have an aerobic exercise that you like that makes you feel better, you can keep doing that.

However, I would only do aerobic exercise several times a week for the fun it could provide, not necessarily for the benefits. If you have fun doing it, it can be great. However, if you want the health benefits and better resilience to stress in a short time as possible, there are better ways.

HIIT

High-intensity interval training (HIIT) gives you a combination of the good effects of aerobic exercise and resistance training in a very short amount of time. It improves your mitochondria; it helps with detoxification and weight loss and dramatically increases growth hormone levels. In other words, it is perhaps the best way to exercise for your health.

In a HIIT workout, you shift between doing high-intensity intervals and resting. For example, you can sprint for 60 seconds and then sit or lie down for 90 seconds. And when I say sprint, I mean sprint. You want to get some real effort into those 60 seconds, so your heart rate rises as much as possible. Because when your heart rate is high, you will get the benefits of aerobic exercise while you're relaxing between the intervals.

However, HIIT doesn't have to be running. It can be anything that allows you to do a high-intensity interval and get your heart rate up quickly. The best thing about HIIT is that it takes very little time. You simply do the intervals for as long as you can, or for a maximum of 15 minutes in total. This means that you will, at most, be doing six sprints or other high-intense intervals.

Furthermore, you only have to do this once a week. Just once a week will give you amazing benefits. You don't have to put more time into it. When you combine HIIT with low-level physical activity throughout the week, your exercise routine will require almost no time, and it will give a whole bunch of benefits. Your resilience to stress should also increase significantly.

Again, it's important to mention that you should always listen to your body. If your fatigue becomes worse after doing HIIT, it might not be the right thing for you at that moment. If that is the case, you can try to do HIIT later when you are less stressed. However, as with resistance training, HIIT should only put stress on your body in the short term, whereas it should increase your resilience to stress in the long term.

Generally, HIIT is very beneficial, and it probably won't hurt you to try it once. You can do one high-intensity interval for 60 seconds and see how you feel the next day or a few days after. If you feel better, you can go for more the following week. If you feel worse, you might want to wait some extra time before you try it again. Recover

When it comes to exercising, the most important thing you can do to minimize stress is to ensure that your body is fully recovered after a workout before you start a new one. If you feel like your body isn't fully recovered after exercising, you should relax or only do some light movement until you're fully recovered.

Nutrition

What one eats directly impacts the way he/she feels? Aim to eat a balanced diet made up of low-fat proteins, fruits, vegetables, and complex carbohydrates. Lessen your consumption of foods that may negatively affect your mood or brain, such as alcohol, caffeine, saturated fats, and foods that have high chemical preservatives level or hormones.

Do not skip your meals. Aim to eat something at least every 3 to 4 hours since going for a long period between your meals might make you feel tired and irritable.

Minimize refined carbs and sugar. You may desire or have a craving for baked goods, sugary snacks, or comfort foods like French fries or pasta, but these foods quickly cause lower energy levels and a crash in the mood.

Concentrate on complex carbohydrates. Increase your intake of foods, such as whole-wheat pasta, baked potatoes, whole-grain bread, and oatmeal as they can enhance serotonin levels without causing a crash. Increase your vitamins intake; eat more leafy greens, citrus fruit, eggs, chicken, and beans. Eat super foods, like spinach, brown rice, and bananas that are rich in nutrients for boosting mood.

Omega-3 fatty acids can also play a vital role in steadying and stabilizing one's mood. Some of the best sources are fatty fish, such as salmon, mackerel, anchovies, sardines, and herring.

When preparing fish, you should bake or grill rather than fry them.

Practice the Power of Positive Thinking

The power behind positive thinking is undeniable. When you think positively:

You receive better results. When you love the new evidence of improvement, you strive further to achieve it continuously

You better notice your flow of behaviors and choices. You are better inclined since you know how you are feeling and thinking.

You create better results, and others in your life respond in favor.

You feel more at ease.

You behave more hopefully, thanks to the elimination of the negative cloud raining over you daily.

You have less time for negativity when embracing optimism.

You allow your mind to be fueled with more positivity, which has amazing effects on your physical, mental, and emotional health.

You are better able to recite positive statements to yourself.

You actively choose to utilize the power of positive thinking each day.

When Faced With a Challenge, Choose Positive Responses

Problems are inevitable and will arise. It is just a part of life. We all face them, but it is critical to our overall wellbeing how we interact with issues. When you negatively react, you end up majorly draining your energy and affecting your health in the wrong way.

Positively facing challenges at hand does not necessarily mean you are forced to be happy about them. It is about learning to choose the best perspective in all situations. We all have a choice of what type of perspective we want, which, in return, affects how we feel.

Here are ways to embrace positivity no matter the scenario(s) you are faced with:

Instead of locking in your first negative thought, ask yourself these questions instead:

What is the situation teaching me?

What is a positive, more peaceful way I can interpret and approach this situation?

Take a moment to breathe and count to 10 (sounds too simple but work **wonders.)**

Take notice of how you are feeling and thinking.

Realize that you can pick your perspective, and nothing can make you think anything. Remember that your mind is a sacred place that is **yours.**

Practice self-love

The bulk of all positivity and the greatness that comes with it begin with you. It has little to do with what is happening in your life and everything to do with whatever is happening within yourself. When you feel good about yourself, it is much easier to jump on the path of positivity.

If you don't believe or love yourself, you are bound to face numerous challenges when it comes to generating a positive attitude that is required for success in life. To help create a better relationship with yourself, you need:

To do something at least one time per week, that is an act of self-care. Think about any action you take to make yourself feel nurtured and supported. Even think about things you do for others or that you do for those you deeply love and start doing similar things for yourself!

To practice the art of forgiving yourself instead of beating yourself up about weaknesses, goals that are unmet, regret, mistakes, the past, or guilt.

To take stock of the things you do love about yourself. Anything from skills, achievements, triumphs, strengths, etc.; Learn to enjoy the journey you have been on so far.

Daily Actionable Steps for Positivity

I became aware of the power that a positive, constant routine played in my life once I honestly started to embrace and utilize it. Here a few things I personally use in my daily positivity routine, plus some others that people find helpful in their day-to-day lives to radiate optimism:

- Regular exercise
- Planning out your day

- Listening to uplifting music that plays a part in motivating and inspiring you
- Praying or having a conscious conversation with life and the universe
- Gratitude
- Visualization practices
- Meditation routines
- Listening and speaking positive affirmations out loud
- "Thought Interruption Technique"
- Jot down recurring negative thoughts
- Write out an alternative idea for each one
- When you are aware of negative thoughts, practice interrupting them and instead, recite the positive thinking to take its place
- Repeat those positive thoughts until it becomes familiar to you
- Choose to end every day on a positive note so that you can capture quality sleep.
- Celebrate every achievement
- Give thanks and learn to be blessed with what you do have in life
- Repeat affirmations that help you feel better about yourself

- Listen to guided meditations
- Journal things that inspire you and motivate you to live a more positive lifestyle
- Ways to Have Happier Thoughts All Day, Every Day

If you learn the power of harnessing positive thinking, you are more likely to attract positive circumstances in life. The same goes for negativity. The more pessimistic you are, the more negative situations will arise. The blessings you receive in your life are ultimately up to you. If you think and act positively, you will then unknowingly call positive things to appear. If you are pessimistic and cynical, you will always be caught up in a whirlwind of negatively self-inflicted prophecies.

Meditation

I was skeptical about meditation at first, but once I started utilizing it in my everyday routine, that skepticism quickly faded. It has been one of the best and one of my favorite methods of removing negative emotions from my life and recovering with a nice dose of positive emotions and spirituality.

Meditation works to rejuvenate your mind, which makes it much more resilient when negativity does arise in your life. It not only rids us of all those bad chemicals, stress, and anxiety in a physical way but in an emotional sense as well.

I like to explain meditation to my readers like this: If you are always wired to be miserable, meditation should be viewed as a big RESET button that allows you to unplug, turn off, and tune out. Meditation is a practice that can be quickly learned and implemented so that when you turn your brain back on, it is now using frequencies of positive thinking instead! Pretty cool, right?

If you use meditation often and long enough, you will discover that a lot of the damage that negativity has caused becomes eliminated, and you are left with a beautiful, clean slate to paint all on your own with your new positive mindset.

Be Thankful

Gratitude, no matter in what context, always has the power to instill more happiness in our lives. Scientifically, it gives our brains a big dose of dopamine, which is a 'feel-good' chemical that erases negative emotions and thoughts.

Mindfulness training

Mindfulness meditation or mindfulness training isn't explicitly a device for cognitive restructuring; however, it's an extraordinary method to prepare yourself to be careful (mindful) of your thoughts when you find yourself lost in them. General awareness of thinking is a fundamental first step in controlling your mind.

Mindfulness training includes picking a focal point of attention like breathing. For a set number of minutes, you center around experiencing the simple act of breathing in order to focus your mind. One of the most accessible breathing techniques to practice is the relaxation breathing, also known as square breathing. Here is how to go about it:

Step 1: Get yourself a quiet spot where you can sit still for ten to fifteen minutes without distractions.

Step 2: Take note of your usual breathing pattern and check how long each inhales and exhales take.

Step 3: Once you have pattern estimation, increment the length of the inward breath and exhalation by one second, basically hindering each inhale and exhale. When you have adjusted to the new, slower rate, add another second to each inhalation and exhalation. If you feel awkward or winded, it likely means you are slowing down too quickly. Proceed with continuously slowing your breath until you are breathing as slowly as you can with no trouble.

Step 4: Once you are settled with a much slower breath, explore by holding after every exhalation and inhalation. These delays can be short, for a couple of seconds, or long, for as long as ten seconds. However long the pauses endure, note you will likely need to alter your pace of exhalation and inhalation to keep breathing without strain, without wanting to pant for air. The strategy is called square breathing because initially, the inhale, the exhale, and the two delays were intended to be of the same length. Similarly, each side of a square is of equal length. Be that as it may, it doesn't generally make a difference, as long as fewer breaths are taken every minute.

Step 5: Set an alarm and proceed with this exercise for ten to fifteen minutes. You will, in all likelihood, experience and increment in relaxation, and a considerable decline in angst.

The square breathing strategy works similarly as the smile strategy: Normally, when we are tense, our body reacts by increasing the breathing rate, and we take shorter, shallower breaths. When we are calm, the inverse occurs. By slowing down the breath, we stunt our mind into thinking we are relaxed, and the majority of the relaxing neuro-synthetic compounds are discharged. Research has indicated that taking part in this strategy has a quick impact on the brain. More significantly, studies have shown that participating in square breathing twice a day has a constant lower level of anxiety in people who are inclined to stress.

At whatever point, any anxiety- triggering thoughts come into your brain, slowly (and without self-criticism) take your mind back to experiencing the awareness of your breathing.

How to Take Control and Choose to Be Aware

Did you know that by simply observing something, you change it? I know that sounds magical, but it's actually backed up by hard science. In physics, this is called the Heisenberg principle. By simply observing a phenomenon, you change the result.

This also applies to what's going on in your head and in your heart. By simply choosing to become aware, you are already starting the process of changing your behavior, the words that come out of your mouth and, most importantly, your emotional, instinctual responses. The best part to all of this is that you're not trying to reprogram consciously. You're not trying to step in there and move things around. You're not purposefully rearranging your mental furniture so to speak. You're not doing any of that. You're just simply allowing yourself to become aware. You're merely choosing to open your eyes to what's going on in your mind, in your heart, and in your logical processes. By observing, you start changing.

Observe Without Judging

Try to observe how certain external triggers bring out specific emotional responses in you. Be aware of the connection. Look at what happens outside of you and trace it to your feelings. Keep focusing on this connection. The key here is to observe without judging. You're not saying to yourself, "This is bad. I shouldn't be doing that." No. You're just looking with curiosity at how certain things bring about particular feelings or specific mental connections. That is the extent of your job at this point in time. Just observe.

Be Your Mind's Most Avid Student

By simply allowing ourselves to be merely an objective observer, kind of like a foreign exchange student who just got dropped into your mind to pay attention and log what they witness, you will be able to see many things that you're normally blind to. The reason why you're blind to them is not because they don't exist, or that they're hard to see. Instead, you are so focused on judging them that you essentially deal with the stimuli in an unthinking way. You only need to see, for example, certain elements, and you automatically conclude that they mean something. You just take it from there. You run with it.

It's not much different from a hunter going to the forest and seeing a big tail with a bushy end and a lot of hair in the center. The hunter hears a growl. The hunter then puts all these factors together and starts heading the other direction at full speed. Why? The hunter organized all this information and came up with the judgment that there was a lion several yards ahead of them. If that hunter kept going in that direction, the lion might end up enjoying a two-legged lunch item.

We tend to do this and, generally, it works for us. For the most part, we're able to save a lot of valuable mental processing time by just simply looking at a tiny fraction of a larger phenomenon, assuming that it means something, and making decisions. The problem is if you want to overcome your negative narratives, you have to connect the dots directly. You have to override your habit of jumping to conclusions.

Connecting the Dots?

Let's just get one thing out of the way. You're already connecting the dots. By and large this is the reason why you're having a tough time. This mental activity is the reason why you're having issues with depression, anxiety, worry, and limiting beliefs which undermine self-esteem and self-confidence. You are doing too much dot connecting.

Now, I'm going to ask you to be aware of how you normally connect the dots and see the gaps there. The reason why you feel that there are certain negative areas in your life is because at some level or other, you're connecting the dots in one specific way. Maybe it's time to reconnect the dots, coming up with new connections and fresh patterns.

Unfortunately, there is no one-size-fits-all formula for this. You have to do it yourself based on your particular set of data. Everybody's triggers are different. Everybody's objective pieces of information are distinct. Still, we all do this. This is one of the few things we all have in common. The difference, however, is that fact that some connections are more productive than others.

You need to look at how you're constantly drawing conclusions from these stimuli based on your narratives. Pay attention to how this choice leads you to act a certain way. After becoming aware that this is going on, start reconnecting the dots. Do you think that you could have a better result if you connected your past experiences and personal narratives with triggers a different way?

See the Overall Pattern of Your Life

The reason why automatic behaviors and seemingly self-regulating emotional states seem almost irresistible is because they are set patterns. We feel we can't escape them. However, keep in mind that you are living in a personal prison of which you yourself are the warden. You're the gatekeeper. You have the keys in your hand. The reason why you're staying in that fixed range of options is because you choose to.

Remember, you chose all these narratives at some level or other. It's like living in a prison, and you have the keys in your hand. You see the keys every single day. In fact, you see them so often that they seem like they're not there. But they're still there in your hand. You could always choose to go about doing things differently.

Your narratives, when woven together, form your lifestyle. We all have a distinct lifestyle-a distinct way of living. It is powered by our narratives.

Is the pattern clear yet? Your normal tendency to connect certain dots and leave particular dots unconnected will produce your lifestyle. Your lifestyle then produces your life. Understand how your personal narratives work through this process. Get familiar with how they flow into each other. Finally, understand how they define you.

The More Aware You Are, the More You Can Change Yourself

Like I said, the great news is that by simply being aware, you start changing things in your life. The longer you observe how you behave and how you interpret certain segments of reality to mean specific things, the more power you will have over your 'automatic' thoughts and actions. The more you understand which triggers unleash certain emotion states and how these lead to certain actions, the more you can change yourself.

Be aware that this is happening. Become aware that you're connecting certain dots. Be aware that you believe specific patterns are true and this defines your identity.

Don't Take Things for Granted

Now, just as you can be looking at a particular phenomenon out in the natural world, it's easy to take certain things for granted. It's so comfortable to think that once you see exact things then it's easy to conclude specific truths.

On the flip side, if you feel that you don't see certain things, then it is okay not to conclude a certain truth. You should stop thinking in terms of shorthand, and instead choose to look at all the things that are playing out in these patterns with a fresh set of eyes. Allow yourself to question everything. Don't just go by assumption.

Don't take things for granted. Don't be fatalistic and assume that there's really not much you can do about the things going on in your life. Don't be dismissive either. Don't think that just because certain things are there, or they're not there, then they don't really mean that much. Instead, look at everything that is happening and see its value. Try to uncouple each element in your assumptions or disconnect it from whatever it is normally attached to, and try to come up with new connections.

For example, if you are constantly triggered by memories of your father because you did not have a good relationship with him, don't automatically recoil at the memory of certain words or phrases from your father.

For instance, my friend Adam was always told by his dad that he was an idiot. Adam rebelled against his father by smoking a lot of weed when he was a teenager. In college, he ended up, doing a lot of drugs. After graduating, he simply chose to coast through life. He didn't have much drive. He didn't really apply himself.

I lost touch with Adam for several decades. Intrigued by CBT, he let me walk him through key memories and coping mechanisms he had. I was able to work with Adam to the point where he was able to take the emotional sting out of the memories he had about his father. When he remembers his father calling him an 'idiot' or saying he's 'good for nothing, he now has a different interpretation.

I worked with Adam to re-interpret that memory as his father challenging him to be better than what he was settling for. Because Adam was one of those "super genius" kids in junior high, he was always easily bored. When a teacher introduced a new concept, Adam figured it out backwards and forwards before the teacher could even fully explain it. That's how quick Adam's mind was. And accordingly, he got really bored easily. And he would always take the easy way out and do as little as possible to challenge himself.

Perhaps his father, when he told Adam, "You're an idiot," was saying that out of love, or out of frustration over the fact that this young person was capable of so much more but constantly contented himself with doing the very least. When we looked at that alternative meaning and we 're-connected' many of his other memories to his personal narratives, Adam's demeanor changed. All that anger and that free-floating frustration that he had with his father started to melt away.

After six months, I met up with Adam again, and he had launched a start-up Internet company that had just been funded a few million dollars. He said to me that our talks about his father had showed him that he could expect greater things from himself. Our conversations changed him, as well as his whole relationship with the concept of ambition and how he defined personal ambition.

It truly blew my mind that Adam had come up with this really amazing idea for a mobile app that is extremely exciting as far as personal productivity and commercial applications go. He had success in him all this time. Still, for the longest time, he chose to interpret his father's statements about him in such a way that it dragged him down, instead of pushing him upward and forward to his fullest potential.

This is what happens when we allow ourselves to avoid being fatalistic and dismissive when we're looking at the dots in our narratives. They may seem like they've been there for a long time. They may seem all too 'natural.' They may even seem logical. Regardless, there are always other interpretations. Never lose sight of these. Don't be dismissive. Don't think that just because your emotional roller coaster operates one way for so long, you're stuck with it.

The Relationship between Cognitive Behavioral Therapy (CBT) and Body Language

Emotional Empath

The most common kind of empathy is an emotional empathy, and it is just what it sounds like. In general, the book you are reading pertains mostly to an emotional empath. An emotional empath will pick up someone else's feelings easily, to the point that you experience them as your own and have difficulty distinguishing the difference between yours and theirs. It is a much deeper emotional sensation, leading to having emotions that don't belong to you, simply because you are near someone who is feeling a strong emotion. The most important thing for an emotional empath is to learn the difference between your feelings and someone else's so that you can better help others with succumbing to emotional exhaustion.

Physical Empath

A physical empath is able to "read" the emotional energy of someone's physical body, meaning that they can interpret what is ailing someone on the physical level. This can be like seeing someone's posture and immediately being able to sense that they have chronic pain in their low back. Some physical empaths choose to work as doctors, healers, and medical professionals because of their skills. Sometimes, this ability will be felt, or "picked-up" in your own body and can lead to chronic fatigue symptoms if you are not aware of your ability to pick up on this kind of energy.

Geomantic Empath

For someone with this type of empathy, they can understand the energy of the environment. This could be like walking into a room or a building and automatically being able to discern the energy of the space. Many people associate this form of empathy with environmental studies and those with an urge to help with ecology and sustainability might be a geomantic empath. Usually, you sense this ability if you either feel incredibly uncomfortable or alternately, incredibly at ease and at peace, in certain environments. It's like "reading the room." With this type of empathy, you will likely feel a deeper bond to certain locations, landscapes, buildings, or places in nature. It is possible, too, that you are sensitive to the historical and cultural history of a certain environment and are able to feel that energy as well.

Horticultural Empath

For this type, it is all about plants and how they "feel." Someone who is a horticultural empath will likely feel drawn to flora and how plants exist in relation to you and the space that you are in. For those who are drawn to working with plants and gardening, you might have this type of empathic tendency.

Animal Empath

An animal empath can feel the emotions of their pets, as well as those of wild animals in nature all around the world. You will likely know just what an animal wants or needs if you have this skill and can offer the pet another kind of support and comfort based on your emotional understanding of their reality.

Intuitive Empath

An intuitive empath can understand something about a person simply by being in their presence. This can come with a lot of practice if you are any of the other kinds of an empath, and it is something that naturally occurs if you are open to your gifts and skills. With this type of empathy, you can usually tell immediately if someone is lying to you, or if they are hiding their feelings behind the words they are choosing to express themselves with. This can create an issue of being too open to others and requires that you understand how to guard and shield yourself well.

We will mostly focus on the emotional and intuitive empath, but all of the techniques and guidelines will be beneficial to any kind of empathy you may have or experience. You can look forward to knowing and understanding all of the various ways that being an empath can be a wonderful gift and before you get further into those aspects of empathy, it is important to look at how there can be challenges to working with this type of emotional availability all of the time.

Understanding the Empath

None of us comes into the world while knowing what empathy is—it is modeled, taught, and learned. It is also something that can naturally occur in the brain function simply because we are all human—and when we see another person in need, a lot of times the urge is to aid them or offer them some kind of consideration.

It begs the question: where does this ability really come from, and how are some people more of an empath than others? There are certainly a variety of ways that these skills can manifest or become a part of someone's regular personality and attitude in life. It isn't just a process of deciding to become an empath and all of a sudden you are one; there is a strong physiological and biological link to your empathic skills, as much as your genetics and early life history and environment play a part.

There is always some kind of debate in the scientific community about what can cause or create certain functions in our brains and thought processes, and in the case of empathy and studying how it works in all of us, there are certainly some specific, neurological causes that form these connections in the mind, allowing someone to comprehend someone else's experience through a form of emotional mimicry.

Other components can also play an important role in your mental and emotional ability to practice empathy— for example, your quality of life as a child. There is the argument of what genetic factors might play a role compared to how you are nurtured and cared for by your family and caregivers. Early life is when you begin to form your personality, and so much of it is impacted by what you are shown by the people in your life. All of the above can be a major force in how someone becomes an empath.

To gain a better understanding of what it can look like from the neurological standpoint, let's learn a little something about mirror neurons and how they can become a part of your brain's ability to understand and practice empathy as an adult.

The Empath and Mirror Neurons

Did you know that your brain is more powerful at computing than any computer in the world today? The 3 lbs of tissue in your skull is a massive machine that can process information in a way that no technology can (at least not yet). The brain is still a mysterious organ that many neuroscientists today feel mystified by as they continue to delve deeply to understand our cognitive abilities and other brain functions.

As with any type of scientific research, the neurological studies that were conducted a decade ago, might not hold sway anymore as we have continued to discover new ideas about what the brain can actually do, through several different studies. Today, scientists are still discovering how empathy works in correlation to your mind matter, and there are a lot of valuable theories that seem to explain some of what can go on in mind to establish an empathic sense.

Recent research in the field of psychology, neurology and empathic studies has looked at the connection between mirror neurons and empathy. The human brain has trillions of neurons, and only some of them are considered to be mirror neurons. These are the only neurons that have been linked to empathic behavior, and as such, have been studied in specific cases to try and understand how empathy really plays a part in your mental cognition and function.

Mirror neurons are located throughout the brain and are not confined to one specific location, so you will find the same mirror neurons in the temporal lobe—where you process language, hearing, and memory—as you would in the frontal lobe, where you produce speech, control motor skills, and solve problems. There is still a lot of research being done to understand how these mirror neurons function and how they are linked to certain aspects of our growth.

Current research describes the following functions of the mirror neurons of your brain:

Understanding Language

This will relate to your ability to learn language by hearing what your parents say to you as a small child, mimicking their words and language to learn it through watching and copying mouth movement, as well as auditory response and reaction.

Imitation

This is an automatic reaction that will often occur starting at a newborn's age when a child will copy, or mimic what the person is doing, such as smiling or sticking a tongue out playfully. Children continue to do this as they get older.

Reading and Understanding Intentions

This relates to knowing when someone wants you to follow their lead, by copying what they are showing you how to do, such as during instruction or class, or if you are a child, being modeled how to use a fork to pick up your carrots. This can also develop into reading someone's emotional or physical intentions without having to use words to understand what is being demonstrated.

Observatory Learning

This is how many people learn new skills and is just what it sounds like: watching someone doing a task and then repeating it, such as watching someone thread a needle and begin to sew, and then mimicking the actions on your own.

Developing Personal Awareness

This is how someone will determine what kind of a person they are, through witnessing or observing someone else's actions and then making a choice to either perform the same action or choose an alternative. An example of this would be watching someone jaywalk, and then deciding to use the crosswalk yourself.

This might all seem so simple, and it is when you think about it, but on a bigger scale, noticing that these mirroring functions are occurring from the moment you are born, determines what capability you might have to perform certain functions as you grow into adulthood. If you are "mirrored" by your caregivers to be unforgiving, disinterested, and incorrigible, then you might not become a very empathic adult.

There is some research being done with regard to mirror neurons and how they are linked to disorders like Autism and that it is possible that Autism could be attributed to a lack of functioning mirror neurons. Other sources have indicated that your early guidance by caregivers and a lack of "healthy mirroring" is what can lead someone to become a narcissist, sociopath, or any other kind of person who lacks empathy.

The research is still coming forward to ascertain what role mirror neurons play in any person's ability to develop empathic skills and our general ability to experience love, compassion and generosity are what set us apart from our animal companions here on Earth. The studies on empathy are certainly offering a gateway to understanding more about this human condition, and even with this knowledge, there is still the process of determining if you are a true Empath, or just acting with empathy.

An empath will have a much more developed, intricate, and complex network of mirror neurons. This is what can cause someone with this natural ability to understand another person's feelings and actions in a much stronger and deeper way. It can help, too, to understand a little bit more about our general identities and how no one is like anyone else.

In the matter of the human mind and our experiences, no two people are alike. We have similarities, we share a lot of our expressions, concepts, beliefs, and values— and yet, with all of this commonality, no one will ever have the same reality as another person. This is because of the quality of your neurological process. Because your brain is formed by your experiences, you will only know your own path of cognition, programming, and other mental function. Your memory is unique to your experience, as much as your dreams are—and each day, everything that occurs will impact your reality in a way that no one else can truly perceive.

That being said, when you are growing and learning, mirroring your world to get an education on how to exist and develop skills, you are tapping into your own mainframe computing system, and the complexity of your mirror neurons depends on so many variables, it can be a challenge to measure without something like an MRI scan.

Mirror neurons grow from infancy and are related to a concept much argued and studied in the scientific communities, and it can help you understand more of the connections between empathy and how it is developed.

One thing that we need to focus on a bit here before we move on is the importance of empathy. This is a skill that a lot of people are going to fail, especially when they start to analyze other people. They assume that everything is black and white and that if someone is showing a certain behavior, the result is the same each time. But people are unpredictable, and they have things that happen that can influence them often without even realizing how that projects out to another person.

For example, if you meet up with someone who has just gotten out of a fight with their partner, they may seem tense. You notice that their posture is tense, their hands are in fists, and ready to punch something, and their speech is tight and angry. If you are not empathetic, and you look at the body signals, you may assume that this person is mad at you when in reality, they are mad at something else.

In some cases, the nonverbal cues you pick up are going to be concerning you and how you affect the other person. But, there are also times when something external, something that has nothing to do with you or that conversation or situation is affecting the other person. Being empathetic will help you to look for and understand some of these things, and can make it easier for you to make that connection with them.

This brings up the question of why we should practice empathy. Some of the best reasons that you should always make sure you are practicing empathy with those around you will include:

You are more likely when practicing empathy to treat those you care about, and anyone else, in the way that you wish that they would treat you.

You will be better equipped to understand the needs of those who are around you.

You will then be able to more clearly understand the perception you create in others based on the actions you use and the words you rely on.

You will be able to understand how some of the nonverbal communication that you share with others is going to impact them.

In the workplace, you will be able to have a better understanding of the needs of your customers.

You will find that it is easier for you to predict, with a lot of accuracies, the actions and the reactions of those you are interacting with.

It is easier for you to motivate those around you if you can look at what motivates them the best.

You can show your point of view to others more effectively.

You will find that it is easier to see a higher resolution of the world around you because you can see the perspective of others and not just your own.

Even when some negativity comes from others towards you, it is easier to deal with it when you understand their fears and the things that motivate them to act this way.

Sometimes, we get so caught up in our little world that it is easy to forget about others and what they are experiencing at the time. Sometimes, we assume they are mad at us, and then we get mad and upset because we don't understand what we did wrong. In truth, if we took a moment to look at what the other person is feeling, and we understood that maybe an outside force that has nothing to do with us is causing the issue, it would be easier to handle that negativity!

Challenge Automatic Thoughts, Dysfunctional Assumptions and Beliefs

10 CBT Instantly Calming Techniques to Change Your Thoughts

There are several tools and techniques currently used in cognitive behavioral therapy in both the therapy context and in daily life. These techniques are evidence-based methods applied to change feelings, thoughts, and behavior and improve the overall life functioning of humanity. The most common tools and techniques of effective CBT practices are outlined below.

Journaling

This technique is applied in gathering the moods and thoughts about someone. A journal technique includes a recording of the time of thought or mood, the source of the feeling or thought, the intensity, how the individual reacted to the thought, among other factors. This technique can help in the identification of thought patterns and tendencies of emotions, describe how they occur, and how to cope, change, or adapt with them.

Unraveling Cognitive Distortions

This CBT technique can be applied with or without the support of a therapist. To unravel the cognitive distortions, one must be aware of the distortions they commonly suffer. This also involves identifying and challenging harmful thoughts that frequently affect someone. The thoughts, which are known as cognitive distortions, are ways that the mind convinces one of something that is not true in the actual sense. Such thoughts always reinforce negative thinking and emotions.

Cognitive Restructuring

After recognizing and understanding the distortions that you hold, you can start to explore how the distortions took root and how you came about believing in them. When you eventually identify a belief that is harmful or destructive, you can start to challenge it. For instance, if you believe that you must earn a lot of money in order to be respected, but you get laid off from your high-paying job, you will start feeling bad about yourself. Rather than accepting this faulty belief, restructuring can help you think about what truly makes someone "respectable."

Exposure and Response Prevention

This CBT technique is typically effective for individuals that are experiencing the symptoms of obsessive-compulsive disorder (OCD). This technique can be utilized through exposing oneself to whatever it is that always elicits a recognized compulsive behavior, but ensuring that you refrain from engaging in the behavior. You can always combine this technique with journaling, or apply journaling in understanding how this tool can make you feel.

Interceptive Exposure

This CBT technique is commonly used to treat anxiety and panic attacks. It involves the exposure of someone to the feared bodily sensations with the aim of eliciting the response. Interoceptive Exposure is intended to help people who suffer from panic symptoms that make them uncomfortable.

Re-scripting and Playing the Script until the End

Re-scripting, and playing the script until the end, is ways that you can work through anxiety by taking control over the anxious thoughts that you are experiencing within your mind. Often, people find themselves experiencing anxious thoughts and struggling to find ways to work through them. Rather than facing the thoughts and letting them play out, they avoid the thoughts and aggressively try to push them away out of their minds so that they can avoid experiencing such tremendous amounts of anxiety. The problem with pushing away or becoming afraid of your thoughts is that you are giving the thoughts more energy and attention than they need. As a result, they grow larger and feel even scarier, and you find yourself experiencing even more anxiety as a result.

If you allow your thoughts to happen naturally and you take a portion of control back, you allow yourself to step away from the anxious experience and instead regain control over your unwanted experience. This can help you begin to experience freedom from your anxiety in a far more positive manner. Using this strategy, you can not only put an end to your anxiety, but you can also put an end to the anxiety that you have about having anxiety, which is often caused by being too afraid to go through the motions of anxiety again.

Actually, engaging in these practices requires you to do two things. For re-scripting, you want to take your time and identify what your thoughts are and why they are not serving you. Then, you want to start telling your story differently. Re-scripting helps you change the course of your thoughts by changing the way your emotions are being felt and observed by your conscious mind. As a result, your emotions may go from feeling overwhelming and scary to feeling reasonable and understood. The more you can lead to you feeling reasonable and understanding, the more you are going to be able to help yourself to improve your response to anxiety.

When you play the script until the end, you can engage in re-scripting at the same time. However, the goal here is also to understand how scary your thoughts actually are by allowing them to play all the way out until the end. Often, we get hung up on the scary part of thought, which results in us continually feeling as though there is nothing we can do to feel better. If, however, we can recognize that we are getting hung up on these scary parts of the thoughts and we allow ourselves to keep thinking the thought through, then we can see that the thought itself is not entirely scary. You do this by asking yourself, "and then what?" until you reach a point in your reality where the scary or anxiety-inducing experience would no longer be such a big deal.

For example, let's say you are scared of public speaking because you are afraid that you will stumble over your words, and people will look at you funny. If you keep getting hung up on this part of the experience, then you might grow incredibly afraid of public speaking to the point that you want to cancel your public speaking engagement. If, however, you instead begin to ask yourself "and then what?" you can start to become aware of what might happen if you were to stumble on your words, and people looked at you funny. Perhaps you would acknowledge that you would keep speaking, and then you would finish the speech and be done. Or, maybe you would acknowledge that you feel embarrassed, take a breath, and keep going. Whatever the script looks like for you, keep seeing it through until you are at the end so that you are more likely to get to the point where you recognize that no matter what happens, it's not the end of the world.

Progressive Muscle Relaxation

Progressive muscle relaxation, sometimes called PMR, is a type of treatment that aligns with meditation and relaxation in one and actually supports people in bringing peace into their body. For people who are experiencing anxiety, PMR can help you release the tension and tightness that you are carrying within your body so that you can begin to feel more at peace. This gives your body the biofeedback of "I'm okay," which leads to your anxiety gradually reducing until the point where it is no longer existent.

You can engage in PMR by essentially focusing on one area of your body at a time and instructing that area of your body to relax. To engage in proper PMR, you want to focus on starting at either your feet or your head, and you want to instruct every major muscle group on the way to your head or your feet to relax. The more you can do this, the more you are going to find yourself experiencing freedom from the tightness and anxiety that you are carrying within your body.

PMR can be done anytime you are experiencing nerves or a busy mind, and it can also be done as a part of a habitual routine to help you release daily stress and anxiety, which is especially important if you are experiencing a generalized anxiety disorder. You can easily engage in PMR on your own, or you can follow a recorded meditation that guides you through PMR if you would like some assistance in navigating this particular relaxation method.

Relaxed Breathing

Relaxed breathing can help you literally breathe peace into your body by taking back control over your automatic responses and relaxing through them. When you are anxious, your body will immediately begin to tense up, and your breath will grow more shallow. You might even find yourself holding your breath if you are feeling particularly anxious, which can lead to even more challenging experiences. If you can take back control over your breath, you can begin to breathe in a deeper, calmer, and more relaxed manner that encourages your entire body to relax as deeply as possible.

Your relaxed breathing can be done on your own or following meditation or guided experience on the internet. These days, many devices like your phone or your smart watch also have breathing apps built-in that can help you intentionally slow down your breath and bring calm back into your body. Following these tools can be extremely helpful in dissipating your anxiety and taking back control, especially if you find yourself experiencing constant and chronic anxiety. Often, seeing the app on your phone or smart watch can actually trigger calmness, too, because you become so used to that particular tool being used to help slow your breath and calm you down.

If you want to do relaxed breathing on your own, you can simply remember an easy breathing rhythm and then intentionally practice that breathing rhythm for one entire minute, or until you begin to calm down, whichever comes last. A great and easy-to-remember breathing rhythm you can use when you are feeling anxious is to breathe in for five seconds, hold it for six seconds, and exhale for seven seconds. These numbers are simple to remember, and this rhythm will help you calm yourself down and begin to experience more peace within your body, mind, and emotions relatively quickly.

Talking to a Loved One

Your anxiety may be your own, but that does not mean that you have to face it alone. For many people, especially those who are facing intense or overwhelming anxiety, having the help of a loved one can be extremely supportive in enabling them to overcome their anxious experiences. You might find that the more you can surround yourself with the support and warmth of loved ones in your life, the more you are going to be able to heal yourself from having troubling anxiety. The reason behind this is that many people succumb to the stigma that anxiety is in any way bad or negative, and so they find themselves experiencing shame and guilt around their anxiety. As a result, they end up holding back and keeping their anxiety to themselves, which can lead to them having even more anxiety.

Suffering alone is not helpful, and it can also lead to you having even more challenging experiences. If, however, you take the time to identify who you can talk to that will be able to respect you and help you and you take the time to work toward actually reaching out to them when you are feeling anxious, you will find yourself feeling far more supported. This way, you no longer feel as though you have to go through anxiety alone, and both you and your support can help you begin to overcome your anxious experiences.

Physical Exercise

When you get anxious, your body produces a large amount of cortisol and adrenaline. Both of these are meant to stimulate enough energy for you to be able to engage in "fight or flight" as needed so that you can safely remove yourself from the situation that you have perceived to be dangerous. If you are not making use of this influx of energy, you will find yourself experiencing a sense of discomfort in your life because this energy can begin to become overwhelming. Rather than being adequately used, it becomes pent up, and you find yourself feeling worse and worse.

If you take the time to engage in physical exercise on a regular basis, it is going to do two things. First, it is going to help you move through that built up energy so that it does not sit there nagging at you and making you feel worse. If you are feeling incredibly anxious, rather than engaging in fight or flight, you can engage in some light cardio or even a more calming form of exercises like yoga or tai chi. Engaging in these types of exercises will help you immediately relieve yourself of the energy that you have built up within you as a result of your anxiety.

Aside from helping you relieve yourself from an immediate bout of anxiety, physical exercise is also going to support you with balancing your hormones and supporting your overall sense of wellbeing. People who exercise on a more regular basis find themselves feeling far more resilient to things like stress and overwhelm, which can be helpful in supporting you with navigating troubling and unwanted experiences with anxiety. This way, you are more likely to feel healthier and more at peace in between bouts of anxiety, and you are more likely to bounce back from your bouts of anxiety with greater ease.

Self-Monitoring DAY by DAY

Avoiding situations that bring you harm is great. But in real life, we both know that that is not always realistic. Life throws plenty of bad situations at you and you can't avoid them all. Therefore, it is essential to develop healthy coping skills for when you do encounter these situations.

Situations that stir up mental illness symptoms can be everyday situations that other, healthier people find to be no big deal. But for you, they can feel catastrophic. They can lead you to relapse in your symptoms, after working so hard to overcome those symptoms with CBT. Learning to cope in harmful everyday situations is essential to keep yourself from falling into despair.

Anxiety

Many everyday situations that are nothing to healthy people can trigger severe anxiety in some. For instance, a huge crowd at an airport can be stressful for anyone, but it can be disastrous for you if you have agoraphobia or social anxiety. But what if you have to fly for work or to visit a sick relative? You have to be a part of that airport crowd, whether you like it or not. The situation is not ideal for you but you can use various techniques to cope with your anxiety.

The best technique is relaxation. Focus on your breathing. Breathe in through your nose, out through your mouth. By focusing on your breathing, you take your mind off of the stress that surrounds it.

Progressive muscle relaxation also is helpful in anxiety-provoking situations. Firstly, start with the muscles in your scalp. Force yourself to relax those muscles. Next move to your forehead muscles; keep roving your mind over your body, forcing the relaxation of each of your muscle groups. The relaxation will calm you and the intense mental focus required to perform this exercise will take your mind off of your stress.

Some people find tapping to be soothing. You can repeat a mantra to yourself such as, "I will survive this. This is really not so bad" as you tap different parts of your body. The physical action of tapping paired with the repeated affirmation can help trick your mind into believing what you are saying to yourself.

Sometimes anxiety can impair your ability to focus on anything. In that case, it is essential to pick a spot on the wall and focus on it intently. Do not chase any other thoughts that enter your head. That spot on the wall is your refuge. Use it to take your mind off of the craziness raging around you and within you.

Conclusion

We primarily focused on cognitive behavioral therapy (CBT) as the underlying platform for solving problems in people's lives. Now, make a list of the most important problems or concerns you'd like to address. Note how often they occur, whether they are relatively minor or quite severe, and how they impact your life. Use the workbook in the appendix at the end. For example, someone may experience feelings of hopelessness. To address this, you could write down that these thoughts occur three to four days a week, that the thoughts are upsetting and intrusive but not so severe that you cannot continue most daily activities, and the impact is that the thoughts take away from your enjoyment of life and make you feel less positive about the future in general.

Depending on how quickly you have read through the content, you may still be experiencing fairly intense symptoms of your emotional struggles despite having read everything. It is important that you do not simply toss it aside and forget about it as you continue to face your daily struggles. Simply educating yourself on what needs to be done will not support you in healing. You will actually need to do the healing work. By remaining devoted and showing up for yourself every single day, you give yourself the attention that you need to truly embrace your healing journey with CBT.

It is important that you truly understand that self-healing does not mean isolating yourself from others. Isolating yourself is a common desire when you are experiencing something like anxiety or depression. However, doing so can impede your healing. Even on days where you do not feel like it, show up for yourself and attempt to make contact with at least one person per day who does not live with you. Doing so will support you in feeling a deeper sense of connection with those around you and will help you feel more attuned with the outside world.

You also need to make sure that you consistently practice your new mindfulness and CBT practices. Even though individuals who recover from psychological disorders using CBT are far less likely to relapse than those who are solely being treated with medicine, you will always be vulnerable to experiencing a relapse in your symptoms. Continuous self-monitoring and keeping yourself well-educated and equipped with the knowledge that you need to combat potential relapses will support you in overcoming them before they become problematic. Even if they do become problematic again, it is no reason to be ashamed.

If you know of someone else who may benefit from CBT. The more that we can spread the message of healing and empower others to discover how they can heal themselves, the fewer people need to suffer from symptoms of anxiety and depression.

Hopefully, we have shown you that the negative outlook on life is merely a negative distortion of thought you can learn to surpass. To support you on your journey towards balanced positivity, we have included numerous exercises and introduced you to a number of techniques that support the mental recovery. You learned how to use the thought record, one of the most important tools to examine your mind and track your progress. By learning how to use the thought record, you will be able to rationally evaluate every stressful situation and challenge that life throws at you. With that in mind, you can use this technique to beat automatic thoughts, rumination, dysfunctional beliefs, and assumptions, as well as to cope with fear and sadness.

Remember to stay open about your thoughts and experiences as much as possible. Communicating with your therapist openly, using detailed descriptions gives them the best insight into your experiences and helps them identify wrong beliefs and assumptions that are guiding your life. You've learned that the most likely cause for you to feel the way you do isn't in the fact that there is something wrong with you, because there isn't, but in the negative core beliefs that have shaped your perception of life. We have explained the definition and examples of core beliefs, helping you to understand how and why the unconscious mechanisms that are guiding you might be dysfunctional. Furthermore, we explained how and why the negative core beliefs cause cognitive distortions, automatic, and intrusive thoughts that are bothering you the most. You now have guidance and instructions to stop nurturing these inadequate thinking patterns and shift towards positivity and clarity.

If your life has been affected by negative beliefs long enough, you may have learned how to use numerous avoidant, self-destructive behaviors. Without knowing it, you were relying on these behaviors to shelter yourself from fear. While avoiding stress might have worked for a while, you are going to have to work past these crippling, self-destructive behaviors in order to grow and change. We introduced graded exposure and behavioral activation as simple but effective techniques for you to gradually and patiently conquer your fears and introduce more enjoyable, positive behaviors into daily life.